RANDOM
HOUSE
LARGE
PRINT

KEEP IT
Pithy

Bill O'Reilly

KEEP IT
Pithy

USEFUL OBSERVATIONS
in a TOUGH WORLD

R A N D O M   H O U S E
L A R G E   P R I N T

Cover design by Michael Nagin
Cover photograph by Visco Hatfield

The Library of Congress has established a Cataloging-in-
Publication record for this title.

ISBN: 978-0-8041-2107-1

www.randomhouse.com/largeprint

FIRST LARGE PRINT EDITION

Printed in the United States of America

10   9   8   7   6   5   4   3   2   1

This Large Print edition published in accord with
the standards of the N.A.V.H.

Contents

INTRODUCTION

First up: Call me clairvoyant, but I know what you're thinking. **Another book from O'Reilly? We have to read yet another book from this guy?** Let me quickly say that this book is not mandatory. This is not something completely different like my works of history. No, **Keep It Pithy** is a literary highlight reel that may help you in your life. I really hope it does.

Over the past twenty years, I have written millions of words. "Bloviating" doesn't even begin to cover it. Eleven bestsellers, thousands of newspaper columns, a daily talking points memo on television, and so on. On my tombstone I want these words inscribed: "He finally stopped talking."

Many publishers have asked me to simply reprint my past stuff. I've always said no. That's because some of what I've written is obsolete. Dated. Not relevant to anything anymore. That happens because life passes quickly and seasons change, to say the least. What was fascinating five years ago may be very boring right now.

But some of what I've put down on paper is worth

another look, especially my predictions about the age of Barack Obama. Back when I wrote the book **Culture Warrior,** I knew little about the man. And what I wrote in **Culture Warrior** had nothing to do with him as a human being. But it did have to do with his mind-set and how his secular-progressive (S-P) point of view was gaining steam in America. Looking back, I see that I am nearly an oracle in this area. It's interesting to read today what I saw in the fictional future that I created years ago. It's also somewhat frightening.

In this book we look back but we also update everything, allowing you to incorporate some of the views I've stated into your own lives should you choose to do that. The only way things will get better in America is for sane people to win the debate. **Keep It Pithy** will help you do that, and it will also clarify things that may be perplexing you at this moment. As usual, I will be blunt and, I hope, entertaining at the same time.

It is especially important for younger Americans to understand what the deuce is happening in their country and how to deal with it so that they can prosper and help America at the same time. Fortunately, I think I have accomplished that in my own life, and I want to impart some guidance so that you can do the same thing. The opening headline is obvious: **Keep it pithy!** We'll tell you exactly why in the pages of this book.

It continues to amaze me that so many of you want

to hear and read what I have to say. It's really the ul-
timate compliment, and I take your interest very seriously. I would never want to let you down in any way.
I owe you honesty, clarity, and my best work. I think
this book will reflect that. Please let me know by email
if it does not.

Finally, I owe a big thanks to my pal Charles Flowers, who has helped me compile the book. You may
have seen the name. Flowers has worked with me from
the beginning of my literary career and coauthored
the book **Kids Are Americans, Too.** Charles is an
interesting story. A southerner with a liberal sensibil-
ity about life, he is an educator and a man of letters.
He and I are about as opposite as two Americans can
get. But we both share a passion for the traditions of
the country and for problem solving. And I think over
the years I have somewhat convinced Charles that the
no spin, pithy approach to disseminating information
is the way to go. He can't admit that to his salon-type
friends because they'd stone him. However, Charles
has reaped other rewards among my fans. They love
him at Peppino's, one of the best Italian restaurants on
the planet.

In this book, Charles and I have selected some of
my best stuff and have presented it in a way that is
designed to help your life. It is another journey that
we hope you will enjoy. And one final thing: Please
keep in mind that in order to move forward, you have
to look backward. We all must understand what has

happened in our lives, in the country, and in society in order not to repeat mistakes and, most important, so that we can find the most moral path to happiness and prosperity.

Life is short. No time to waste. Here now—the pith!

State of the Union

ONE

JUST AS I PREDICTED AND LONG BEFORE WE HEARD OF PRESIDENT OBAMA

The Growing Success of the Progressive Agenda

Back in 2006, I had fun imagining in my book **Culture Warrior** a future State of the Union speech by a U.S. president named Gloria Hernandez. Here's a summary of that imaginary pol's goals and philosophies:

A sharing of the wealth by targeting the affluent for most of the government's revenue . . . lax school discipline on American children to promote their so-called liberties . . . naked hostility to religious values and their expression in public . . . a "one-world" approach to foreign relations that would prevent the U.S. government from imposing a policy that would benefit America first . . . a touchy-feely vision of our society that places individual self-expression and rights over self-sacrifice and adult responsibility.

Did I get it right? Well, I made one serious mistake. I imagined that this would be the platform of a president elected in 2020. Looked at a calendar lately?

———

The brilliant men who forged the Constitution understood that Americans should have the opportunity to pursue happiness without much government interference. They also believed for both moral and practical reasons that the greater good must always take precedence over individual selfishness.

The S-P notion that the U.S. government has the right to seize private property (which is exactly what the estate tax achieves, for example, but under stealth wording), or redistribute legally earned income from the affluent to the poor, runs counter to the founding spirit of America in every way.

Look at the evidence. The United States became the strongest nation on earth because individuals working their butts off created a unified powerhouse.

———

Right now our national slogan is "The more you make, the more we take. And we're not even going to watch how we spend it."

———

Throwing our tax dollars away has become the new national pastime, replacing baseball!

———

Usually, as I've noted in the introduction, I'm not likely to disagree all that much with what I've opined in the past. Exceptions are notable, and I will note them. Most of these quotes from my writings will require no explanation. My core values have not fundamentally changed.

Too late now!

———

In fact . . .

Politicians will argue—as many have on my program—that the government needs your money. This is a lie. There is more than enough tax revenue available today to pay for the armed forces, roads, police, and other vital services without looting the take-home pay of working Americans. No, the reason our taxes are so punitive is right there in front of you: obvious and arrogant wastefulness in government-run programs. Forget the $400 toilet seats in the Pentagon budget—peanuts. The real killing waste is in programs that do not work.

(I then noted the "horrific failure" of Clinton's $30 billion drug war and the $200 billion his administration threw at public education, to no great effect.)

I could give you hundreds of examples of ridiculous government waste, but that would take a whole other book. Right now, I have enough on my hands trying to write this one. But you can trust me on this: The tax situation in this country is brutal, including the fact that your elected representatives and their opponents are using entitlements to buy votes. That includes Social Security, Medicare, and Medicaid. Listen very carefully when pols talk about these hot-button programs. Are they making sense, or are they pandering? **You** have to decide. The bottom line is that few government programs are run effectively or with discipline. What we call "waste" or "pork" is **reelection insurance** to our leaders. Besides, the prevailing wisdom is that there will always be more tax money coming in, so don't sweat it. Is it time for another tea party like the one given in honor of King George III in Boston Harbor? I'll meet you at the water's edge. . . .

———

Welfare has failed. Public housing is a shambles. Public education is a mess. The poverty rate remains almost unchanged. And yet the Big Government Beat goes on.

In 1766 Benjamin Franklin warned the British Parliament that if the stamp tax wasn't repealed, the colonies might well revolt. Today our tax situation is revolting (sorry), but too many of us remain passive in the face of it. The road to hell is paved with good intentions—and you know what? Those intentions are being paid for big-time by all working Americans. It is enough to test even the strongest person's sobriety.

———

I don't expect any help from the Fifth Estate.

The sad truth is that most high-profile media people are looking out for themselves and themselves alone. On any given day in Manhattan, you will see them dining in incredibly expensive restaurants with other powerful people. You will see them at swanky parties and black-tie charity events. You will see them at their lavish vacation homes in the Hamptons, Aspen, or Loudoun County, Virginia. You will not see them at Wal-Mart.

———

The split between "we" the people and the media is especially severe in the spiritual arena. A survey by the American Society of Newspaper Editors shows that the rate of atheism among journalists is about 20 percent, significantly higher than among the general population, where it stands at about 9 percent. When one in five media warriors does not believe in the existence of a supreme being, it's not hard to figure out why many press people support secular causes like unrestricted abortion, gay marriage, and restraints on public displays of faith.

———

Hard work and discipline lead to economic success. Government handouts and unsupervised policies of pity only rob people of incentive. If tax money continues to be wasted, it becomes morally wrong for our government to confiscate huge percentages of income and property from Americans, even if they are wealthy.

———

Until the mid-1930s, America was a nation that basically said to its citizens: "Your forefathers have given you freedom, so good luck, see you around, hope you make it." Then came the Great Depression, World War II, the Great Society, the Age of Aquarius, the Me Generation, and finally the anything-goes Clinton years. Throughout those generations everything changed. While John Kennedy once asked what you would do for your country, modern politicians were suddenly lining up to tell you what they were going to give you, and one of the biggest entitlement pushers around was JFK's brother Senator Edward Kennedy. Most giveaway programs have been complete failures, but the rhetorical battle continues to this day.

———

To this day, I keep these lessons close:

1. Work hard.
2. Keep a clear head. [That means avoid getting hammered as much as possible.]
3. Don't compromise when you know you're right.
4. Give most people the benefit of the doubt.
5. Don't fear authority.
6. And definitely have a good time.

———

Chances are you're not wealthy.

Because in America very few people are. That's the deal. The average annual pay in America is about $43,000 for an individual, about $63,000 for a household. And the celebrated or maligned "1 percent"? In 2012, $343,927 a year would put you in that group. So . . .

If you don't believe class is important in your life, you might want to ask yourselves some questions like these:

- Did my spouse or I turn down a chance for another job because of the fear of "not fitting in"?
- Did someone in my family not stand up for himself or a family member after some injustice because he didn't feel he was good enough?
- Do I miss out on some social or sports activity I like because I'm afraid everyone else involved in it dresses better or has more income?
- Have I discouraged my children from chasing an ambitious goal because I'm afraid they won't be happy or comfortable in an upper-class situation?
- Do I refuse to learn something—Alpine skiing, computer skills, wine collecting, field hockey— because I think that other people are already way ahead of me and I would be acting "above my station"?

The class situation has not improved over the years.

Don't expect it to change in our lifetimes.

Live with it and make your own way.

Even people of modest means can have class.

———

I'm reminded of conservative humorist P. J. O'Rourke's definition of the three branches of government: not the legislature, executive, and judicial system we learned about in school, but "money, television, and B.S."

―――

If I'm right about secular-progressivism in this country (and I am!), we shouldn't just roll over and submit. . . .

We have the right to vote. People have died to protect that right. But half or more of us stay home during important elections. When we talk to pollsters, we reveal amazing ignorance about the issues, the candidates, and even the structure of government.

Who represents you in Congress? And is he or she a Democrat or Republican? What's his or her stand on abortion, gun control, trade with Communist China, taxes . . . ? You'd be surprised at how many Americans haven't a clue to the answers to questions like these. And if you're surprised, I'm amazed. These people make the laws that define our lives, and they decide how to spend the money collected by a confiscatory tax system.

Clue: Were tax hikes an issue in the last national election?

Another clue: Did the election results affect the decisions made to avert the so-called fiscal cliff?

Crazed ideologues on the right who laugh off environmental concerns are just as stupid as crazed ideologues on the left who have somehow determined that human life in the womb is expendable.

Just as with global warming, no one knows exactly when life begins. Only the deity knows. You can **believe** anything you want, but you DON'T KNOW. We do know one thing, however: Scientists have proven that upon conception, human DNA is present. Get it? The fetus already has the codes in place from its biological mother and father. So the "mass of nonhuman cells" argument goes right out the window if you're an honest person.

In my opinion, the "compassionate" liberal cadre that supports abortion on demand—for any reason at any time—is guilty of gross human-rights violations. Worshiping at the altar of "reproductive rights" is wrong. Abortion should be rare, regulated, and discouraged. Human dignity demands it.

So you can see that the bold, fresh guy has some problems with both sides of the ideological spectrum. But unlike Judy Collins, who sang about not knowing life at all, I am more confident in my views. Independent thought based upon greater good, realism, and, yes, compassion drives my agenda and dictates my analysis.

———

More on taxes in today's political climate . . .

Politicians take your tax dollars and give them to their friends and patrons. How corrupt is that? Well, they get away with it because politicians know that you won't notice that you're being stiffed as long as the malls stay open late and your cable system provides twenty-four-hour sports coverage.

In other words, the political climate in the USA has changed in favor of the crooks and incompetents. How can you guarantee yourself a future in public service? Be willing to sell out for campaign money. And if you're an especially talented liar, you can go very far. Both major parties would be happy to have you join the hustle. (But get in line quick. It's only the first few who will be allowed on board. Any more than that, and the bandits get nervous.)

Am I being too harsh?

Simple answer to that: no.

———

But there are, and have been, exceptions.

The politician I most admire is Abraham Lincoln. The reason is simple: He was kind. He showed his concern for everyday Americans while trying to lead this country through its greatest crisis so far. Failure to act wisely and courageously at the height of the Civil War would have destroyed the nation, which was founded at such risk barely a hundred years before.

Even so, Lincoln devoted one day a week to reading mail from the people and answering with notes on the reverse side of the page. Not surprisingly, many letters were written to seek jobs or other favors. The president often tried to help these ordinary people, even though they were strangers to the corridors of power and influence. . . .

I have seen a number of these letters from mothers who wanted to visit their wounded sons, from older men who needed work to support their families after all the young relatives had gone to war, and from children worried about their fathers in uniform. Lincoln's replies are amazingly compassionate. He reveals himself as a great man who used determination and humility to save the Union. Neither vain nor vengeful, he had no spin guys or bagmen and took no money. Because he loved his country, he suffered greatly at the loss of life on both sides of the conflict. Despite the tremendous personal stress and the nationwide chaos, Lincoln still helped individuals while working to keep the country whole.

Where are today's Honest Abes?

Dunno, but we should keep an eye out. Might happen again.

The above sketch was written years before I wrote my recent bestseller, **Killing Lincoln**. Good in the world is too often matched by evil, as in the person of the assassin John Wilkes Booth.

———

Am I serious about that observation?
Yes.

Evil is a constant presence throughout the world. I've seen soldiers gun down unarmed civilians in Latin America, Irish terrorists kill and maim their fellow citizens in Belfast with bombs, and heroin addicts with AIDS knowingly share needles with other addicts without telling them about the infection. Evil.

Once, I stood in the cellar of an abandoned Italian church that had been used by Satanists in rituals that included murder. The feeling of evil permeated this room. I had never felt anything like it.

But then I felt it again in Africa at Victoria Falls in Zambia. I stood where human sacrifice was practiced years before by tribes native to the area. Victims were tossed off the cliff into the thundering falls. I got out of there quick.

So I know that true, unrepentant evil exists. And I firmly believe it will be punished, just as good will be rewarded. That is part of the order of the universe, if we only take the time to recognize it.

TWO

I'VE QUESTIONED EUROPEAN SOCIALISM FROM THE BEGINNING

Hello France, Next Stop—God Forbid—Greece!

Europe is on such an economic roller coaster that no one, certainly not your humble servant, could reliably predict what will be going on when this book comes off the presses.

Chaos? Collapse?

Don't point your finger at any one or two countries alone. The whole European way of thinking about social and economic matters has been a shared lunacy and a dangerous misreading of human reality.

You only have to travel to Europe to see the difference that an entitlement culture makes. While the United States is a vibrant, creative, and exciting place, Europe today is largely stagnant. Workers there have little incentive to move ahead, because the rate of taxation is punishing and the governments guarantee a certain standard of living. In France, young people demonstrated for weeks because the government wanted a new law that would allow employers to actually fire them during the first two years of employment if they screwed up on a regular basis. But nooooo, we can't have that! The French sense of entitlement basically says, "You owe me prosperity, government. You owe me."

Yes, this was written before 2008.

All the more reason why Europe is in such deep trouble even as President Obama seems to be taking us exactly in its direction.

Is it inevitable that America must head down this road? Not by a long shot. Keep in mind this discussion I had with the good Dr. Charles Krauthammer on **The Factor** after some college students at UC Davis went wild over a tuition increase:

O'REILLY: The irony here is that some of those students want America to be an entitlement society, but when the money runs out as [it has] in California, they run amok. . . . Charles, how bad do you think the entitlement society in America is right now, and is gonna get?

KRAUTHAMMER: Well, judging from those young people, who appear rather agitated that they are not having their college education subsidized enough, I say it's getting out of control. Because remember, who pays the taxes that support their college education? Three quarters of Americans have no college degree. I think the answer to your question is a little bit complex. I think the majority of Americans don't want to give up the entitlements they already have, but I think the majority of Americans don't want to add onto it, and to become like a European social democratic society.

O'REILLY: Now why is that? Because the taxes then rise so high that individual achievement is robbed and that the American dream shrinks because you just don't have the cash to do it because you're giving the government the cash. Is that the reason?

KRAUTHAMMER: That is the reason, and what we had was a spontaneous uprising, if you like.

A peaceful one, of course, in the United States. The Tea Parties, the town hall meetings . . . all said very loud and clear, "Yes, we like our Social Security but we are not going to add onto it with a new healthcare entitlement. We know we're going over a cliff with taxes and debt, and as a result we want to stay where we are, stay Americans with some protections. We're not going to get rid of the New Deal, or even the Great Society or Medicare, but no new stuff." And that's what the fight over healthcare is all about.

O'REILLY: It is. It is about that and about smaller versus larger government. However, the younger people that we saw out in California, they have a different view when you look at the polling about healthcare. The younger the American is, the more likely they are to support it. So that tells me that the new generation wants the government to be a nanny state.

KRAUTHAMMER: Except that the new generation is going to get older. And they're going to have a family, and they're going to have kids, they're going to have payments, they're going to have a mortgage and they're going to pay taxes. And they won't like the taxes. Those kids out there aren't paying a lot of taxes. And as they become adults, they are not going to have the same political attitudes as they had at eighteen, when you're wild, you're free, and subsidized.

O'REILLY: Why do you think people in Scandinavia, who are just about the same as Americans—Scandinavians come here, there's no difference basically—why do you think they want the nanny state in places like Sweden? Not Norway so much, but Denmark, Sweden, France—France isn't in Scandinavia—what is the mentality that Western Europeans have that they want to be taken care of?

KRAUTHAMMER: Well, remember they're not the same as us because it was the more independent ones, the ones who didn't like the strictures of government, the regulations, the religious oppression, who came here. This spirit of being independent and not wanting to be controlled by the government is something that is intrinsic in America, it's the essence of America, it's what distinguishes Americans who are essentially refugees of the old society in Europe. That's why it's always been harder to make Americans break to the yoke of government as happened in Europe. Once you get accustomed to the kinds of entitlements that you have in Sweden, England, France, elsewhere, it doesn't get undone. And America is different—it's resisting the imposition of new yokes. And that's what's happening today.

That's what we have to remain vigilant about—remembering that America was forged in independence, and not for government to impose its will like in so many European countries. This is such an important fight for our future.

THREE

MINORITY REPORT

The Obstacles, the Search for Answers, and the Case of the Sharpening Divide

Old white men may be becoming fewer and fewer at the ballot box. That's arguably a numerical minority down the road, and we'll see what that means for traditional America soon enough.

But the historical meaning of "minority" in this country is a shameful, often brutal story. We have to admit that.

The sad truth is that for more than two hundred years most black Americans were systematically deprived of the right to pursue happiness, and Native Americans were brutalized as America was being settled. Thus, the government today does owe African and Native Americans, and the poor in general, more attention and specific entitlement programs to help level the playing field. On that most traditionalists and S-Ps can agree.

Surprised?

You shouldn't be.

Key words: "to help level the playing field."

———

And the playing field is as tough today, in many cities, as it was when I began working as a TV news reporter long, long ago.

Cops and prosecutors know that it's impossible to enforce the law in any neighborhood if there is not cooperation between the people who live there and the authorities. In rich neighborhoods, most people love the police. They wave at them and smile and give them Christmas presents.

All is fine between the police and the citizenry.

Not so in the ghettos. Suspicion and animosity exist between the police and many poor people, and each side has valid reasons for the distrust. The cops know they are disliked, and they know the streets are dangerous. The folks know the police are sometimes resentful of the danger and hostility they face—and that resentment sometimes spills over into unpleasant confrontations, even with law-abiding citizens. Fear is present on both sides. And fear will always cause hostility.

———

Violent crime and drug dealing in the nation's minority precincts are often completely out of control. The police who patrol these areas are sometimes frightened and always on the defensive. They are tense, and this often leads to aggression and poor judgment. We are talking about human nature here, not institutional racism. Members of the left in America are often well intentioned, but they are just as often clueless. There will always be corrupt and racist cops because there will always be corrupt and racist people. But police officers on the street get up every day knowing that they might not come home at night. And for this they should be given the benefit of any doubt.

———

I know this much to be true: It is not easy being a minority in the United States. Not only are you outnumbered, but the crushing weight of irrational ignorance is, generally speaking, directed toward you far more than it is at the majority. Sometimes whites in the USA overlook racial bias entirely because it does not affect them.

———

I never got the antiblack thing. New York Giants center fielder Willie Mays was my guy even after the

team moved to San Francisco. Cleveland Browns running back Jim Brown was actually from Long Island. I idolized these men. So when some adults threw the N-word around and mocked blacks, I had a hard time processing it. If all races were cheering blacks on the field—and they were—why would anyone deride that race after the game? The anti-black crew in the neighborhood could never answer that simple question.

———

I'm sometimes asked why I do so much reporting and analysis of minority issues, and my reply is brief: because few others do and all Americans deserve equal justice and a fair chance at the pursuit of happiness. The elite media are literally scared speechless of offending minorities in America and thus shy away from most confrontational reporting on situations that injure those who do not have the resources to fight effectively for themselves. For all of the politically correct rhetoric you hear or read in the press, little is actually being done to right wrongs on the tough side of town.

———

There is, of course, hope. Many local leaders in besieged neighborhoods are trying to improve things. But for real change to happen in chaotic neighborhoods, there must be rules, strict rules. There must be a code of conduct that is widely accepted in the inner cities, just as there is in the affluent suburbs. Here is a creed that might be a place to start:

Having a child out of wedlock would be considered a harmful thing, something to discourage.

Drug selling would be considered a violent crime, and those involved in this most harmful of enterprises would be shunned and reported to the authorities through the churches.

Drug addiction and alcoholism would be considered contagious diseases. Those afflicted would be encouraged to get help but not looked upon as victims.

All kinds of child abuse and neglect would be confronted by the community immediately and reported to the proper authorities. There would be zero tolerance for adults who hurt or endanger kids.

Police would be assigned to provide protection at all public schools and would be stationed on campus to deal with disruptive and destructive students, as well as disruptive and destructive outsiders. [As in Newtown, Connecticut.]

Curfews on teenagers would be enacted and enforced by local communities.

Zoning laws would be toughened and standards of care imposed on properties both public and private. Run-down buildings would be more easily condemned and then sold at auction to responsible builders.

Public nuisance laws would be passed so that individuals who disrespect neighborhoods and properties by actions such as graffiti, public lewdness and intoxication, incivility in words or deeds, littering, or the general creation of mayhem could be arrested and prosecuted by local authorities.

If that kind of creed was encouraged in all poor neighborhoods, and a cooperative discipline imposed by responsible citizens (who are the majority in every neighborhood), you would see the ghettos of the country gradually transformed into solid working-class enclaves.

———

The class system as related to race plays a role: Single-income white households have a median income of $39,000, while single-income black households have a median income of $25,000. And the earnings gap between rich and poor is widening.

And ever widening still.

This is not a minority problem. This is a national problem.

All people who work deserve a fair chance and the respect of the community.

That is the American ideal, and I don't want us to forget it.

———

The suggestions listed above might make even more sense in light of the following observations from my **Culture Warrior:**

Although 89 percent of blacks voted Democratic in 2004 [it rose to 95 percent in 2012], when it comes to social issues African Americans are largely in the traditional camp. A Pew Research Center poll taken in July 2005 found that 75 percent of black Americans believe secular-progressives push too far in keeping religion out of schools and government. Only 17 percent of African American voters want to legalize gay marriage—an overwhelming statement of traditionalist conviction. . . .

Because the African American political establishment is largely locked into one issue—advancement of blacks through government largesse—African Americans remain largely on the sidelines in the culture war. Generally speaking, taking up the battle is simply not relevant to them, because traditionalists have not defined the culture war to coincide with their interests. I believe that is a huge mistake.

In many black communities, Christian churches are prominent centerpieces. Faith is an important tradition in black America. That's why the gay marriage issue is overwhelmingly rejected by blacks. Their religion says homosexuality is not acceptable, and many African Americans bitterly resent the argument that marriage for homosexuals is a civil right. If you want a lively discussion, walk into a black church and put that on the table. . . .

Take another issue: drugs. Many African Americans have seen firsthand what narcotics can do; they don't want hard drugs legalized. Lawlessness and the breakdown of the traditional family in poor black neighborhoods (the out-of-wedlock birthrate for blacks is 70 percent) have deepened the cycle of poverty and deprivation. Any sane person can see that.

And older African Americans generally deplore the rise of gangsta rap and the disintegration of civility among some young black people. This is a big [Bill] Cosby theme, and he pounds it home in his lectures again and again, despite attacks on him by the S-P community, which

often views the hate-filled rap lyrics as "genuine expression." . . .

The upshot of all this is that it's safe to say few, if any, citizens are enlisting in the S-P corps in East St. Louis or South Central Los Angeles. But, again, not many blacks are waving the traditional flag, either. It would take a strong black leader who understands that the Judeo-Christian tradition, as well as a return to discipline and personal accountability, would greatly aid the advancement of African Americans. Until such a leader arrives, most black Americans will remain disengaged from the culture war that is raging around them. And that's a shame.

FOUR

RELIGION UNDER ATTACK

Who Cares? You Can Hear a Pin Drop

Your religious freedom means that I can't tell you what to believe.

My religious freedom means that you can't stop me from talking about what I believe. Just don't listen, if you don't want to.

I have often written about my faith; it's a large part of who I am.

As far as your personal religious conviction, that is completely up to you. But I will say this: Used in the correct way, religion can be a force that makes your life more worthwhile. It can make the bad times bearable and the good times more satisfying. Spirituality looks out for you because it brings you out of yourself and into a realm where the welfare of other people becomes as important as your own. . . . That kind of worldview will allow you to build relationships with people who will indeed look out for you even as you are looking out for them.

And now for the completely ridiculous . . .

Why did the word "Christmas" suddenly become controversial? Why did I have to spend quality TV time on this issue? . . . The answer is the semi-successful perversion of the U.S. Constitution. The ACLU and other secular-progressive groups constantly say they are challenging public displays of Christmas and other spiritual expositions to **protect** Americans from the emergence of a "theo-

cratic" government—that is, a governmental system driven by religious thought and judgments. The tired "separation of church and state" argument is used again and again to justify attacks on spirituality in the public square.

But the "separation" argument is one big lie, a bogus piece of propaganda cooked up by an intentional misreading of the intent of the Constitution.

This "wall of separation" falsehood has, however, been lovingly embraced by the secular media and foisted upon the American public with a ferocious intensity.

Please trust me when I tell you that, just a few years ago, I never envisioned being a culture warrior on behalf of Christmas. To me, Christmas has always been the most magical time of the year. I remember as a small child sitting on the stairs early Christmas morning before anyone else was up, staring down at the scene before me. Santa Claus had come! All the presents were neatly wrapped and perfectly placed under the tree (a real one). I was mesmerized. What treasures would my sister and I be getting? I just sat there and soaked it all in. I remember the moments vividly. Why would **anyone** want to mess with Christmas?

But in recent years, the traditions of Christmas began to be portrayed in some quarters as somehow "controversial," which really teed me off. So, in the fall of '05, I set out to alert the nation that Christmas traditions were under siege and behind the action was a well-thought-out S-P campaign to marginalize the national holiday (which was almost unanimously approved by Congress and signed into law by President U. S. Grant on June 28, 1870).

Night after night on my TV program, I presented the evidence: Giant retailers like Sears (and others) had banned the mention of the word "Christmas" in seasonal advertising. The Lowe's Company told its store managers to sell "holiday" trees, not Christmas trees. The city of Boston changed the name of its

Christmas tree on the Common to "Holiday Tree." (It was changed back after Mayor Thomas Menino intervened.) There were scores of other examples. . . .

[Simply put, the ACLU began targeting Christmas. They lost in court on several occasions but won in the long run because small communities were intimidated by the expense of fighting the group's lawsuits against various Christmas displays, including a visit from Saint Nick. . . .] Eight out of ten of us in America are Christian and celebrate Christmas as a "religious occasion." But in the interest of inclusion I suggest that we allow the S-P movement to celebrate their version of Christmas. Let's call it "Feel Good Day." And a Happy Feel Good Day to you!

While the religious aspect—Christianity—is certainly in the forefront of the Christmas controversy, the political agenda in the war on Christmas has remained largely hidden. It is a decidedly covert operation, in other words. In fact, many people were surprised when I said on TV and radio that politics, not religion, was the driving force behind the attempt to keep Christmas behind closed doors.

Here's my explanation in a nutshell: Almost every social change the secular-progressive movement wants to achieve is opposed by religious Americans. Therefore, the more the S-Ps can diminish religious influence in America, the faster their agenda can become a reality. For example, the S-Ps are furious that gay marriage initiatives keep getting voted down, even in the most liberal states, and believe that the primary opposition comes from organized religion rallying their flocks to oppose homosexual nuptials with sin-based arguments. . . .

So, for the S-P agenda to succeed, religion in America must be deemphasized, just as it already has been in Western Europe and Canada, where secular-progressives have made huge gains. . . . Goal number one is to secularize the American public school system in order to drive children away from religion and into the S-P camp. And what is the most wondrous display of religion worldwide? Why, Christmas, of course. Little kids seeing a manger display just might develop a curiosity about this baby Jesus person. What's this Christmas deal all about, anyway? There is no danger of that happening with winter solstice or with a holiday tree. Is there?

With no moral shield, millions of American kids will fail. . . . The secularists don't care; they want children to be at the mercy of a materialistic society and a greedy media. They want kids to rely solely on parents who are often irresponsible and self-destructive. Right now all we can do is pray for the kids and fight the secularists hand to hand.

And if you want some empirical evidence to back up that opinion, listen to this: A study of college students seeking psychological counseling has found that their emotional difficulties are far more complex and more severe than those observed in the past. Researchers at Kansas State University studied students from 1989 to 2001 and concluded that those seeking help for depression doubled during that time period. Also, the percentage of students taking some type of psychiatric medication increased twofold.

That trend is not limited just to Kansas. In a 2002 national survey, more than 80 percent of 274 directors of counseling centers said they thought the number of students with severe psychological disorders had increased over the previous five years.

Now, you can argue all day long **why** this is happening, but I'll give you one huge reason: Many young Americans simply do not have a force in their lives that can relieve their emotional suffering. They are drifting away from our religious traditions—and religion can be that force, at least in part. If you are able to believe that a higher power will look out for you and will balance bad times with good times, your stress level will not get out of control. Religious faith is generally bad for the "shrink" business, but honest mental health workers know what's going on. "People just don't seem to have the resources to draw upon emotionally to the degree that they used to," the director of counseling at the University of Nebraska, Dr. Robert Pomeroy, told the **New York Times**. "What would once have been a difficult patch for someone is now a full-blown crisis."

The rise in dysfunction parallels the rise in secularism, no question about it.

———

There's a reason that the cross is the symbol of Christianity. It is a powerful statement that a good man suffered for me, that a just God was looking out for me, and if I lived a good life, I would be rewarded after death. Those beliefs, sincerely held, can get a human being through many hard times. . . .

I believe that a concentration of believers has made America a strong, noble country. As I got older and learned more about history, I saw how the Founding Fathers used Judeo-Christian philosophy to forge the Constitution, perhaps the most perspicacious political document ever designed.

———

In our personal lives, we do actually enjoy full freedom of religion in this country. But publicly that is no longer so in America. Because of the rise of secularism, a philosophy that argues there is no room for spirituality in the public arena, religious expression in public is under pressure from some in the media and, of course, from the intolerant secularists who hold power in many different quarters. They are **definitely** not looking out for you.

One of the biggest frauds ever foisted upon the American people is the issue of separation of church and state. The American Civil Liberties Union, along with legal secularists like Supreme Court justices Ruth Bader Ginsburg and John Paul Stevens, are using the Constitution to bludgeon any form of public spirituality. This insidious strategy goes against everything the Founding Fathers hoped to achieve in forming a free, humane society.

I said "fraud," and I meant it. Let's look at some historical facts. There is no question that Benjamin Franklin, Thomas Jefferson, James Madison, and most of the other framers encouraged spirituality in our public discourse. Letters written by these great men show that they believed social stability could be achieved only by a people who embraced a moral God. Time after time in debating the future of America, the Founders pointed out that only a "moral" and "God-fearing" people could meet the demands of individual freedom. That makes perfect sense, because a society that has no fear of God relies solely on civil authority for guidance. But that guidance can and has broken down. All great philosophers, even the atheists, realized that one of the essential attributes of a civilized people is a belief that good will be rewarded and evil will be punished.

In 1781, Jefferson said the following words, which are engraved on the Jefferson Memorial in Washington: "God who gave us life gave us liberty. Can the

liberties of a nation be secure when we have removed a conviction that these liberties are the gift of God?"

I wonder what Jefferson would think of the ruling by the Ninth Circuit Court of Appeals in California that the word "God" is unconstitutional in the Pledge of Allegiance. I also wonder what ol' Tom would think of the American Civil Liberties Union suing school districts all over the country to ban the use of the word "God" in school-sanctioned speech. Here's how ridiculous this whole thing is: At McKinley High School in Honolulu, an official school poem has been recited on ceremonial occasions since **1927**. One of the lines mentions a love for God. After the ACLU threatened a lawsuit, that poem was banned from public recitation, a seventy-five-year tradition dissolved within a few weeks.

This is tragic insanity. To any intellectually honest person, it is apparent that the Founders wanted very much to keep God in the public arena, even uppermost in the thoughts of the populace. What the Founders **did not** want was any one religion **imposed** by the government. Jefferson, and Madison in particular, were suspicious of organized religion and of some of the zealots who assumed power in faith-based organizations. But the Founders kept it simple: All law-abiding religions were allowed to practice, but the government would not favor any one above another.

At the same time, Jefferson in his wisdom predicted that some of the things he and the others wanted for the new country would eventually come under fire. On September 6, 1819, he wrote: "The Constitution . . . is a mere thing of wax in the hands of the judiciary, which they may twist and shape into any form they please."

How prophetic is that?

[The ACLU's] true agenda is a secular society. So my question is: Where are the countersuits? Where are the voices of opposition to secularism? Right now they are found primarily on the Christian right, which has been demonized, pardon the pun, as fanatically extreme because of its tendency to condemn its opposition to hellfire. Believe me, I know. Many letters to **The Factor** give me clear road maps to the devil's den—and suggest I'm headed there.

The unrecognized bitter truth about God and America is that organized religion is scared. The churches don't want to say anything that might endanger their tax-exempt status. They stay out of politics; they actively practice the doctrine of separation of church and state. But that doesn't mean that good people who believe in the presence of public spirituality have to stay out of the fray. As the Isley Brothers sang, "Fight the Power."

———

Nowhere is the civil impotence of religion in the USA better demonstrated than by the Catholic Church. A whopping 65 million Americans are Catholics, almost 25 percent of the population. Yet the Catholic Church in America, which used to be a tremendous force for effective social change, is now on the defensive and, in many quarters, is an object of public derision.

Do you know why? Because the Catholic Church stopped looking out for the folks, that's why. Its leadership is made up primarily of elderly white men who have spent their lives playing politics and currying favor with the conservative zealots in the Vatican. Cardinal Law in Boston, Cardinal Mahony in

Los Angeles, and Cardinal Egan in New York are all men of guile, power players who enjoy their wealth and influence. I could list scores of bishops who play the same kind of callous game—that is, amassing power and money while completely forgetting the mission that Jesus died to promote.

[And there's more. On January 21, 2013, after continuing pressure from potential prosecutors and litigants, the Los Angeles Archdiocese finally released thousands of pages detailing the cover-ups of abuse in the mid-1980s. Supposedly, that could be only a portion of what will eventually be made public. In one case, an internal disciplinary file of a predatory priest showed that he was protected even after disclosing the rape of an eleven-year-old boy and sexual abuse of as many as seventeen other boys.

What will happen to the retired cardinal and others involved in this sick enterprise? Perhaps nothing at all. Legal experts say that prosecution is very unlikely because the statute of limitations that applies has run its course.]

With such leadership, it should come as no surprise that the clerical sex scandal broke wide open. With a few exceptions, like Archbishop Sheehan in New Mexico and now Phoenix, Catholic leadership in America is made up of venal, self-absorbed men who embrace the daily philosophy of "cover my butt." When Cardinal Law learned of abusive priests, did he leap up in outrage, throw out the perverts, and call the cops? No, he did none of those things, according to his own sworn testimony. Instead, he kept the situation quiet so it wouldn't hurt his standing in Rome. Thus his solution to child molestation by his priests was to pay the victims off and have them sign a nondisclosure agreement. Then he'd send the priest to rehab and reassign the pervert when he got out so he could be pronounced "cured." That policy, of course, led to the brutalization of hundreds more children, but did Law care? He dodged and weaved and attacked the press until finally the evidence became so overwhelming that he was publicly humiliated. **Then** he said he was sorry. But even after the crimes and payoffs became public, the Vatican refused to take aggressive action against Law and the other perversion enablers. And so the reputation of the Catholic Church in America arrived where it is today—completely down the drain.

The devil and his disciples are thrilled with this series of events, and Jesus must be weeping. He commanded his followers to seek out afflicted children and comfort them. Did Cardinal Law miss that lesson? And what about Pope John Paul? Where was his outrage? In fact, the Pontiff even refused to meet with some of the sexual abuse victims when he traveled to Canada in 2002. . . .

The self-destruction of the American Catholic Church leaves the field wide open for the antispirituality forces to march in and do what they will. With the Church now lacking in any moral authority outside its own core, the loudest argument in town belongs to the freedom-**from**-religion spokes-people. And they are winning big.

———

My last word on religion is a practical one based on timeless logic: If you live your life subject to the rules of Judeo-Christian tradition (or Buddhist, Islamic, or another religious tradition), then you will do more good than harm on this earth. You will love your neighbor and help other people out. You will not do things that hurt others or yourself.

So, if everyone was religious wouldn't the world be a much better place in which to live? Of course it would. And if there is no God at the end of it all, what does it matter? You're in the ground or scattered to the winds. If the deity is a fraud, you won't possibly care. You're gone.

But while you're still here, the real trick is to live a successful, positive life.

———

To this day, I still go to Sunday Mass. Often, it's boring. Many times the priest goes on far too long about the mustard seed. Hey, Father, those of us showing up on Sunday have got that down, okay? Fallow ground is not good. Let's advance the discussion, can we?

In helping me to determine right from wrong,

good from evil, and trying to correct injustice, my Catholic faith is invaluable. In public and on TV and radio, I usually keep my religion to myself, because I have a secular job; I'm a journalist, not an evangelist. But if somebody brings up the subject, I tell him or her what I just told you.

Religion has been a very positive thing in my life. Without it, I would never have been motivated to expose bad guys and celebrate heroism. Most media people are self-interested and cautious. But I see my job as much more than a big paycheck and a good table at the bistro du jour. I am on a mission.

FIVE

FROM 9/11 TO BENGHAZI

What Have We Learned About the War on Terror? Anything?

Our U.N. ambassador, Obama buddy Susan Rice, recently crowed that the United States has "decimated" al Qaeda worldwide. (Misusing the original meaning of the word—look it up!—she evidently meant something like "destroyed".)

Really, Madam Rice?

It seems that many in government still are unable to read the handwriting on the wall. Like a virus, terrorist beliefs, goals, and actions have spread from the Middle East into other parts of the world. Attacks here at home—so far foiled—are no longer infrequent.

Have we learned anything at all?

The secular-progressive movement opposes coerced interrogation—not torture, but harsh treatment—of captured terror suspects. They object to detention of them at U.S. military prisons like Guantánamo Bay. In addition, the ACLU opposes military tribunals (rather than civilian trials) to determine the guilt or innocence of suspected terrorists, floating wiretaps (already in use in U.S. criminal investigations), telephone surveillance of overseas calls by U.S. spy agencies, airport profiling, the Patriot Act, the war in Iraq, and random bag searches on subway or mass-transit systems.

In short, the ACLU opposes making life more difficult for terrorists but proposes absolutely nothing to make Americans safer. Osama has got to love it.

And for too many years, he did.

But the debate about the usefulness of harsh interrogation techniques rages on. Have you seen **Zero Dark Thirty**? Brilliant drama, but it is not going to change the minds of those on either side of the argument.

———

A very peculiar response to the terrorism on 9/11 crossed into the field of religious controversy.

If you haven't heard about a certain required reading list at the University of North Carolina that erred in the interest of "diversity," you're going to be shocked, puzzled, or both.

I was distressed to hear that in the fall of 2002, the administration at UNC was going to require all incoming freshmen to read a book entitled **Approach-**

ing the Koran: The Early Revelations. The book is a sanitized version of Koranic philosophy, concentrating on lyrical stories and poetic lore. It's a very interesting book, but there's no way it should be mandatory reading in any public school.

Just imagine the outcry if any school demanded that students read **Bible Highlights** or **Nice Stuff from the Torah**. I mean, the ACLU would be setting itself on fire in protest—figuratively speaking, of course. But the ACLU was strangely mute when UNC issued its reading list.

So what was **really** going on here? Well, the backlash from 9/11 was hurting many law-abiding Islamic Americans, and the philosophy of "diversity" was taking some hits. So the University of North Carolina decided to set a proactive example and require students to read a book that is favorable to Islam. The intent was good, but it was a direct violation of the separation concept because it required students to learn about the positive aspects of a specific religion while ignoring the negative aspects. That's religious advocacy, not intellectual discipline. And that's not allowed in a publicly funded university in the USA.

The force behind the Islamic reading selection was UNC professor Dr. Robert Kirkpatrick. On July 10, 2002, he entered the No Spin Zone on **The O'Reilly Factor**. I've condensed some of our debate, but the main points are these:

O'REILLY: The problem here is that this is indoctrination of religion.

KIRKPATRICK: No, it has nothing to do with that. It's a text that studies the poetic structure of the Koran and seeks to explain why it has such an effect on two billion people in the world.

O'REILLY: UNC never gave incoming freshmen a book on the Bible to read.

KIRKPATRICK: We assume that most people coming to the University of North Carolina are already familiar with both the Old and New Testaments.

O'REILLY: But if you did do that, there'd be an outcry all over the country.

The professor had no answer for that. Soon after, under pressure from the North Carolina legislature, UNC dropped the book from its required reading list. **Approaching the Koran** became an optional reading assignment, as it should have been all along. I'll go one step further: If the book was mandatory reading in a theology or history class, I would have had no problem with it. But forcing all incoming freshmen to read any book praising a specific religion does violate the mandate that public universities have to live by in order to receive tax dollars.

There's an interesting side note to the controversy. As I said, the ACLU was MIA during the UNC brouhaha (I love all those initials). Also, most other media did not cover the story as aggressively as we did. As part of our analysis, we rejected the idea that reading the Koran book would help us get to know the world that the 9/11 killers inhabited. Number one, I don't think the revelations of the Prophet Muhammad have anything to do with homicide and terrorism. And second, I reject the argument that you have to digest a book of poetry and religious interpretation in order to "know" your enemy.

I said this to Professor Kirkpatrick: "[As a UNC freshman] I wouldn't read the book. And if I were going to the university in 1941, I wouldn't have read **Mein Kampf** either."

Kirkpatrick asked why. "Because it's tripe," I answered.

The next day a number of Muslim websites wrote that I compared the Koran to **Mein Kampf,** the usual vile propaganda some of these sites spew out. What can you do?

Here's the key question: How can terrorism exist if rational human beings know that murdering innocent women and children is the most cowardly act on earth? The answer is complicated, but, in the end, it comes down to untreatable mental illness. Osama bin Laden and his crew are not discernibly different from Hitler, Mao, or Stalin. Shrinks define them as sociopaths, but that is a clinical term for the hospital or classroom. In the everyday world, these men are simply evil and must be isolated or killed so that innocent people can be protected from their treachery.

But, Lord, there are so many of these barbarians. There are millions of human beings who have killed or will kill people because they believe some god or the führer or whoever has ordered that. If you still resist the idea of active evil in the world today, just picture the nineteen 9/11 hijackers killing three thousand people for absolutely no reason. Time after time, history has shown us that this kind of murderous conduct is part of the human condition. But still, some on this earth refuse to believe that evil exists and that terrorism is the epitome of it. Getting people to understand that truth is central to the struggle of our times.

Bottom line: Terrorist killers and those who support them are evil. Period.

State of Yourself

" 'Tis himself!"
—Traditional greeting when a flamboyant
individual enters an Irish pub

SIX

WHAT'S MINE?

Americans Just Want More Stuff, and That's a Problem

And I'm looking in the mirror here. . . .

Here's something that really surprises me: The more stuff I have, the more stuff I want. And so I looked around and saw that everyone else was the same way. It was not until I had a few things that I noticed how this works. The material stuff is addicting!

Remembering my parents, I try to fight against the "stuff addiction." I refuse to buy jewelry or trinkets. I don't need expensive toys like Jet Skis or snowblowers. I keep the material things **under control,** and I banish thoughts of them from my brain. Besides, I am very busy. My life doesn't include window-shopping or paging through mail-order catalogs by the pool or jaunts to compact disc stores or Home Depot. These are all invitations to spend money unnecessarily. . . .

Greed is the destroyer of success. You cannot be creatively successful and greedy at the same time. I'm talking about both material and emotional greed here.

Sorry, Wall Streeters. No apologies to you guys.

Note to Hillary Clinton. Why keep coming up with more government programs to give our tax money away, when you could teach us all how to make a fortune on our own? You invested $5,000 with Robert "Red" Bone, a commodities trader later under investigation for allegedly manipulating the market, and got back profits of $73,000 a few days later. Tell us your secret, Hil, and we might vote you senator for life!

Change that offer to "president"?

The **most** ridiculous part of our American system is this: Different rules apply to the rich guys.

It's not supposed to be that way, right? Our country was designed to be "for the people." **The** people, not the **rich** people.

In short, this country has developed a ridiculous blind spot: the power and glorification of money.

This is truly an affliction. It is holding us back as a nation, as a community. The true heroes of America are not the new Internet billionaires or the overpaid sports stars and movie actors or the wise guys who jack up their companies' stocks. The true heroes of America are the men, women, and teenagers who go to work for a modest wage, fulfill their responsibilities to their families and friends, and are kind and generous to others—because that's the right way to live. . . . The working people of the United States are the most important ingredient in the enduring American story.

But the rich and powerful have forgotten or never learned that bedrock truth. Or they simply don't care.

———

But forget them.

Each of us is, to a large degree, in control of our own lives.

That includes me; that includes you.

Why is there so much drug and alcohol abuse in America today?

Simple: Alcohol and drugs make huge profits for legal and illegal organizations.

Simple again: Much of the population is bullish on intoxication . . . ["I want mine"]. And set in their ways. Dedicated pot smokers believe they are "mellow" and look down on crackheads nodding out in alleyways or deserted basements. Young professionals sniffing coke know that they're on top of the world, masters of the universe: The drug tells them so. The country club set, knocking back martinis and Manhattans and Cosmopolitans, looks down on the rednecks at the noisy beer joint across the county line, and the writers and intellectuals at the local college sneer at both groups for being "alkies" but believe that a trip on the latest psychedelic drug is an intellectual adventure. But everyone has one belief in common: I can handle my "drug of choice."

Here's the takeaway: If you are after success in America, substance abuse can be your downfall.

Some of the drugs may have changed since I wrote the above, but the moral is the same. Self-indulgence, and especially harmful, debilitating self-indulgence, is not going to give you what you want. It will keep you from getting what you want.

———

But it's not that simple. Do you know anyone who is "just saying no"? I hope you do, but I have several reasons to doubt it.

Try these (the stats have changed since 2001, when I printed this list, but the story line is much the same):

1. There are in excess of 10 million "heavy drug users" in the United States.
2. Approximately 70 percent of street crime is drug related.
3. Approximately 70 percent of all child abuse is committed by substance abusers (this includes those who abuse alcohol).
4. There are more than 1 million DUI arrests annually in the United States.

And now, voters in several states, as we saw in the 2012 elections, think that it's "bitchin'"(if you recall

that word from California in the late sixties) to legalize marijuana.

———

There are three basic strategies needed to control
America's drug problem. First, impose coerced drug
rehab on all criminals who are arrested and test positive for narcotics. Second, use the U.S. military to
assist the Border Patrol from Brownsville, Texas, to
Imperial Beach, California, and use the Navy to assist the Coast Guard. And third, sentence major and
persistent drug sellers to banishment in faraway federal penitentiaries. . . . Back in the 1960s my father
told me that anyone who dealt dope was a parasite,
a person beneath contempt. I always remembered
that. How many children are being told that today,
especially in the ghetto neighborhoods? What do
kids think when they encounter the sleazy dealer?

SEVEN

THE KIDS

Hollywood Sleaze, Wrongheaded Educators, Nutty Judges, and Other Problems Knocking on the Door

The assault on traditional values is especially insidious when various elements of society, from entertainment to the schools, from advertisers to judges, ambush our kids at school, on the playground, or over broadcast media and the Internet.

Where to begin?

How about 2006?

For the secular-progressive movement to achieve its goals in America, it must undermine traditional parental authority and convince children there's a brave new world out there that does not include being raised in the traditional way. The S-P goal is to diminish parental authority, which, in the past, had been unquestioned.

This is a strategy—mentally separate children from their parents—that has been practiced by totalitarian governments all throughout history. In Nazi Germany, there was the Hitler Youth. Chairman Mao created the Children's Corps in Red China. Stalin and Castro rewarded children who spied on their parents. That's the blueprint.

If you want to change a country's culture and traditions, children must first abandon them and embrace a new vision. Hello, secular-progressivism in the USA. I'm not saying these people are little Adolfs; I **am** saying they have adopted some totalitarian tactics in their strategies.

———

I want you to recall how the courts can weigh in on the S-P agenda.

Kids seven to ten years old in Palmdale, California, were required by the school district to take a very disturbing sex survey. Sample question: "How often do you think about sex?" That's not a misprint, folks. You can read the whole story in my book **Culture Warrior,** pages 124–27.

But here's the pith:

The parents sued the district in federal court. [The case went up to the Ninth Circuit Court of Appeals, the most liberal federal court in U.S. history.] . . . Judge Stephen Reinhardt wrote the unanimous opinion, which stated that parents of public school children have no fundamental right to be the exclusive provider of sexual information to their children. Reinhardt was direct: "Parents are possessed of no constitutional right to prevent the public schools from providing information on that subject to their students in **any forum or manner** they select. . . . No such specific [parental] right can be found in the deep roots of the nation's history and tradition or implied in the concept of ordered liberty."

That noise you hear coming from underground?
It's the sound of the Founding Fathers rolling in their graves.

———

Remember "Captain" Lou Albano, the wrestler? He always said, "This stuff is fake. Don't try it at home."

So listen to me, someone whom you know from TV, when I say, "Be careful what you let your kids watch, and what they start to believe, if they fall for everything they see on TV."

It started back in the fifties. . . .

The parents gave up part of their job to TV, TV brought in pretty pictures of perfect family life, and the kids glued to this mental bubble gum began having **unreasonable** expectations of their own human, unscripted parents. Most parents want to do what's best for their kids, though it's not always easy to know what that is. With TV images and ad temptations millions of American parents came under siege. TV, according to one writer, "fed a sense of generational superiority" in the kids who watched it. I know exactly what he means, and so do you. . . . Satisfying the desires of children can be an overwhelming task. Worse, it can distract parents from paying attention to the really important parental duties: teaching discipline, morality, and the truth about how the world works.

Or, in the same vein:

Seven in ten [high school students] admit to cheating on tests, and 92 percent say they lie. And most of those kids don't feel much guilt at all. . . . What caused this deplorable state of affairs? Number one, "cowardly parenting." Number two, "corrupt national leadership." As the tree is bent, so will it grow. And today kids can look all around at so many bent adults that they can hardly guess what it means to be straight. People basking in the spotlight—and I don't mean just politicians—are forever presenting terrible examples to the children of America.

And if we so-called adults can be tricked senseless by the clever shills of Madison Avenue, pity our poor children. The ads are designed to make them think that they are the most deprived creatures alive because they don't own expensive designer clothing or high-tech toys and games. . . .

Money doesn't buy love or happiness. We have to help our children understand that the proof of affection is **not** an overpriced gift. Otherwise, we are helping the advertisers set them up for a frustrating life of trying to cope with their problems by racking up credit card bills at the mall.

The late Steve Allen talked about the dangers of TV to children on my program some years ago.

I think it's a conversation worth remembering:

O'REILLY: Do you think that watching these programs will make kids want to have sex?

ALLEN: No. Mother Nature makes them want to have sex. The argument is that when sexual material is dealt with on television and nobody has to worry about birth control or sexual disease, then the implication is, "Hey, it's all kind of cute and hip and let's do it even though I've never met you before."

O'REILLY: So you believe kids are impressionable enough to pick up a message like "They're having fun at Beverly Hills High. I should have fun at my school"?

ALLEN: Yeah, I believe that. There's a lot of documentation. This is not just some theory of mine. I am by no means a saint. But the sleaze and vulgarity on TV disgust even an old roué like me. It's part of the whole dumbing down, the coarsening. The question is, what kinds of parents are the kids today going to make? I think the answer is, not too good.

O'REILLY: Why?

ALLEN: Well, imagine an ideal father. Would you like it if he came home with a couple of broads on each arm? You see that image on TV.

O'REILLY: Are you referring to President Clinton?

ALLEN: That's another matter. But really, if people don't know we have a problem here, then we are in worse shape than I thought.

———

But neither Steve Allen nor I would ignore the challenges that parents face today. No guilt trips here for working parents who must sometimes, for economic reasons, put their children in the care of others.

Look at today's reality in America. Families have to deal with a tough dance card. The cost of housing and modern conveniences is significant, and taxes are gutting the take-home pay of the working class. By necessity, most Americans have to work longer and harder than they might like. If you have more than two children, chances are both parents will have to work at least part-time. . . .

Children need a calm environment, focused attention, consistency, and discipline. Working parents can provide those necessities if they are willing to engage and stimulate the child when they are at home. Day care is risky, no doubt about it. Exposure at a young age to undisciplined or troubled children at a center can cause angst in your own child. The bacteria count in some of these places is off the chart and the supervision is out of your hands. The gently smiling caregiver might be a simpleton who sets the kids down in front of a TV and does little else. Not a great situation any way you slice it unless you get lucky. There are excellent day-care facilities but if your kid is in one, make sure you drop in unannounced from time to time. . . .

[No one] has the right to make working mothers feel guilty. American women have pursued careers and raised fine families at the same time. However, these dual purposes must be carefully thought out and executed with precision. Children should always get first priority, and if trouble develops, the job has to be put aside.

Torture movies are flooding the market, especially in the summer, when young people are looking for something to do. These cynical films revel in explicit scenes of human suffering inflicted with a cavalier glee by both the actors and the special-effects people. Sadism rules, and some sociologists believe a diet of this stuff desensitizes people, making them less likely to sympathize with the real-life suffering of others. So, are the people profiting from torture movies evil?

The torture-film people don't have a tortuous explanation for their abysmal behavior; they have a simple one: It's only a movie. What's the big deal? Everybody knows motion pictures are fiction; there's nothing real about the pain and suffering gleefully inflicted on-screen.

Except it's sickening.

If you think about it, the torture industry is very easy to explain. Simply put, it makes a product for sadistic people to enjoy. The more suffering on-screen, the better. Let's get a close-up of that arm being amputated and that eyeball being gouged out. Again, it's all about money. Why else would any-one spend time and resources filming ways to hurt people? Where is the good in that?

The answer, of course, is that there is no good in that. Only evil. Simply put, anyone who delights in portraying or watching human suffering is sick. Got it?

———

Another topic on which the media are no friends to family values: drugs.

Until public pressure forces our apathetic and fright-ened politicians to get really tough on those who sell narcotics, Americans will continue to die with needles in their arms, prostitute themselves, infect each other with the AIDS virus, and steal anything they can. How much heartache has to pass through the nation before society reacts? Are you going to wait until it's your child with the drug problem?

As for the media, their delayed reaction and their lack of responsibility have been, generally speaking, disgraceful. If the stars aren't flaunting their own

personal drug use (Willie Nelson, Snoop Dogg), they are participating in projects that glorify drugs and alcohol (and cigarettes, for that matter). Movies have made brilliant use of charismatic stars and flashy cinematography to make the drug world look lucrative and normal. Business as usual, babes ahoy.

One such project is the movie **Blow,** starring Johnny Depp and Penelope Cruz, two attractive actors who directly appeal to young people. The film is based on the life of convicted cocaine dealer George Jung, who is currently serving twenty years in prison.

Before the system finally caught up with Jung, he smuggled drugs for more than twenty years, supplying thousands of tons of cocaine to millions of Americans. He accumulated millions of dollars that he spent on himself. Women threw themselves at him. The Jung party was constant and unrelenting and the movie documents all of it.

What the film does not address is that many people became hooked from using Jung's stuff. How many people died or became crack whores or gave birth to addicted children because George Jung was in business? Hollywood was not interested in that tale.

Here's a paragraph that caught the attention of many of you who have read my books. It must have struck a chord, especially with parents:

Money spent wisely can buy you personal freedom. With enough money you can ignore unreasonable demands and avoid humiliating financial situations. **They** won't be able to control your life. Don't waste your money on foolish material cravings, like the silly gas-guzzling SUVs littering your neighborhood. No, money can help you fulfill your potential as a human being: **Earn it, save it, and then shut up about it.**

You guessed it: Many readers discussed this paragraph with their kids.

What percentage actually got the message through? No stats on that one . . . but it never hurts to try.

I like to call this strategy Operation Elevation. Here's how it works: From the time your children can comprehend complete sentences, make clear that you and your spouse expect behavior that is better than the norm. Because they are special, they will be held to higher standards of conduct. In other words, you are elevating their self-image by persuading them of their self-worth.

And when they see other kids harming their bodies by drinking, smoking, taking drugs, or engaging in irresponsible sex, explain that these losers do **not** value themselves highly. They're doing themselves in because they're unhappy about their lives; they don't feel popular enough or attractive enough, so they fall for the short-term illusion of substance-induced kicks or cheap sexual thrills. Continue to emphasize to your kids that their behavior should reflect the special status they have in your eyes.

Just in case you need to ask, we do indeed follow that rule with our kids in the O'Reilly household.

It's not hard to do, because we don't have to fake it, and neither do you. Each parent should believe his or her kids to be special, "better than the norm."

———

The government cannot legislate decent parenting. Any clown can have a child. There are no tests, standards, or guidelines for parents unless they violate the child abuse or neglect laws. Therefore, some children will be so traumatized by their upbringing that they will cause society big problems that we all pay for, sometimes with our lives.

So what does society do?

Again, it all comes back to the free will that I believe we all have. Even though a child has it rough, there will come a time when he or she, like all other human beings, is faced with a clear choice: Either become a productive citizen or become a problem. Almost every violent criminal I've ever spoken with had a terrible childhood. But if society, out of some misguided compassion, does not hold them accountable for harming others, then the result is anarchy.

As you know, some well-intentioned liberals disagree, arguing for lenient sentences and "rehabilitation," even for heinous child rapists. But that point of view is both dangerous and unfair to both innocent kids and law-abiding adults. The government's first obligation is to protect its citizens, not empathize with those who would harm them.

———

History clearly demonstrates that without structure and accountability, human beings have a tough time staying on the rails. And children must be taught this over and over again: An effective person must incorporate discipline into his or her life, and a just society must demand responsibility from its citizens.

———

When your child reaches eighteen, it's all over. You've done your job; the ship is launched. You can hope that you've raised someone who will join the forces of good in America, not a candidate for an entry-level job in the porno industry. It won't be long before your own son/daughter and daughter-in-law/son-in-law are having their own children, probably, and looking around at the world of malls, media, and mass-market culture in a new light. Now it's their turn.

With any luck you can relax and have fun again. You've been **chaperoned** for years, if you think about it.

The above image is idealized, of course, especially in these uncertain economic times. You might be taking care of a grandchild, your son or daughter might have to live at home longer than either parent or child would want, or a severe illness might deeply affect your family dynamic.

But the basic ideal still holds, I believe. Whatever challenges you and your family face, those eighteen and over should be doing their fair share as adults. That's how you raised them.

———

While we're thinking about our kids, let me remind you that I once threw the floor open to a kind of made-up debate between two very famous and strong women:

RIDICULOUS NOTE: Chief White House "enabler" Hillary Rodham Clinton wrote that "it takes a village" to raise children. My parents and their friends thought that it takes parents. They were sorry that some of my friends had maniacs for parents, but they didn't interfere. And they didn't want anyone poking their nose in our house, either.

THIS JUST IN: "Discipline is a symbol of caring to a child. He needs guidance. If there is love, there is no such thing as being too tough with a child. A parent must also not be afraid to hang himself. If you have never been hated by your children, you have never been a parent" (Bette Davis, **The Lonely Life,** 1962).

Well, Bette might be overacting here, but that was her job, right?

———

Many of us are deeply conflicted about our parents. My father and mother certainly provided for me and made damn sure I got educated and was taught the essentials of life. But can I say that my father was always looking out for me? No, I can't. My mother's instincts were much more in that direction, but my father had demons that intruded on his parental duties. As with millions of other American parents, my father set a terrible example by inflicting unnecessary pain on his children. He did not do this on purpose. He simply could not control himself.

———

Where you stand on the following might indicate what kind of parent you are.

Just saying . . .

So here's the deal with this ridiculous "educational strategy." The schools can't or don't teach some kids anything, but, according to the law, the kids have to go to school, even if they're a pain in the rear end. If school authorities insist that they either learn something or be held back, the kids will be around that much longer. So, to get rid of them as quickly as possible, teachers promote them through the system and allow them to graduate with a high school diploma. I've seen kids holding a diploma they couldn't even read. This is just great, isn't it? So now these kids are released into the world not knowing how to make change. That's why you see electronic cash registers that have pictures of products instead of numbers on the buttons. Worse, these kids have been taught one lesson very well in their twelve years of so-called schooling: They are not going to be held accountable for failure. When you have a lot of people believing that, you're in real trouble. Did you wonder why the USA has more people in prison than any other free nation in the world?

———

Now for something really disgusting.

And we'll meet our old friends at the ACLU on the sidelines.

The welfare of a child means less today because of the promotion and acceptance of certain so-called special interests. The most notorious example—and I am not making this up—is an organization based in the United States called the North American Man-Boy Love Association. It advocates the legalization of sex between men and boys as young as **eight** years old. Read that sentence again and digest the eight-years-old part. This vile NAMBLA group was formed in 1978 and calls for the "empowerment" of youth in the sexual area. It says it does not engage in any activities that violate the law.

Oh yeah? What about the fact that NAMBLA was involved in funding an orphanage in Thailand that allowed grown men to rape and molest the children who lived there? And what about the case of child rape in Ohio, where NAMBLA was found guilty of complicity in the crime? The Ohio Court of Appeals ruled that NAMBLA's literature, found in the possession of the rapist, showed "preparation and purpose" in encouraging the rape.

It gets much, much worse. A NAMBLA member recently raped and murdered a young boy in Massachusetts. In October 1997 ten-year-old Jeffrey Curley was playing near his home in Cambridge when two men tried to lure him into a car. When he resisted, Salvatore Sicari and Charles Jaynes got brutal. They wound up killing the boy and then drove to Maine, where they dumped the boy's body in a river.

Both men were eventually arrested, convicted, and sentenced to life imprisonment. Prosecutors at the trial produced as critical evidence a diary kept by Jaynes. In it he flat out stated that he became obsessed with having sex with young boys **after** he joined NAMBLA. How did the organization allegedly poison him with its ideas? According to the diary, Jaynes received NAMBLA literature in the mail and visited the group's website on computers at the Boston Public Library. Clearly, these NAMBLA people wanted to get their message out. According to lawyers familiar with the website, it actually posted techniques designed to lure boys into having sex with men and also supplied information on what an adult should do if caught.

Jeffrey Curley's parents are suing NAMBLA in federal court for $200 million. And guess who is defending NAMBLA in the case? Can you spell ACLU? That's right. The most powerful free speech watchdog in the world is using its money and re-sources to make sure that NAMBLA is not driven out of business. Is this an outrage or what? . . .

Their rationale: "Regardless of whether people agree with or abhor NAMBLA's views, holding the organization responsible for crimes committed by others who read their materials would gravely en-danger our important First Amendment rights."

Baloney! I respect the ACLU's goal of protecting the rights of all Americans. At their best, this group is courageous in defending legitimate expressions of opinion, some of which, like the Nazi marches [in Skokie, Illinois], are pretty vile. But NAMBLA is a different matter because the freedom to harm chil-dren is not built into our Constitution.

For the record, the Curleys dropped their lawsuit in 2008. Only one witness came forward to testify against NAMBLA, and the judge in the case deemed him incompetent.

NAMBLA's website, as of this writing, is still up and running.

You don't want to go there, I'm guessing.

And now there is much, much worse out there, facilitated by the Internet, where perhaps millions of child pornography consumers are actively posting, downloading, and creating this smut, perhaps photographing the abusing or rape of a young member of the family.

Much of the horror was reported in an aptly titled article, "The Price of a Stolen Childhood," in the **New York Times Magazine** of January 27, 2013. As writer Emily Bazelon documents in shocking detail, the youngster may have to live with the photos or videos for the rest of his or her life, even after the pornographer is arrested and sent to prison. The material continues to circulate. Often the older child is recognizable to those who view or distribute the pornography. The damage is worsened by the knowledge that the images are still circling the globe. It can be seen, as one judge has put it, as "continuing digitized rape."

Here's the thing: We parents can never be too careful. We don't want to freak our kids out by imagining the worst at all times, but we have to keep our eyes and ears open, especially when we hear the gentle hum of computers behind closed doors.

———

And so let's sum up with my Ten Commandments of Effective Parenting, which I first brought down to the world exactly a decade ago in my book **Who's Looking Out for You?**:

1. A parent who is looking out for you will make time for you if he or she possibly can. Hint: Serial golfing is no excuse.

2. All punishments will fit the crime. Discipline is essential, but no parent should inflict frequent physical or mental pain on a kid. Childhood is supposed to be a wondrous, joyful period. Parents are the grown-ups and have to be patient, within reason. Words can deeply wound a child. Parents must display kindness and understanding. Corporal punishment should be a last resort, and used within guidelines that have been clearly established before any physical punishment is administered.

3. Parents who are looking out for their children will be under control in the house. There will be no random violence, intoxication, sexual displays, uncontrolled anger, or vile language (sorry, Ozzy Osbourne). The house should be a refuge, a place where the child feels protected and loved. If it is a chaotic mess, the parents are not looking out for the kids.

4. If a parent is looking out for the child, he or she will educate that child in the best possible way. That includes paying college tuition if at all possible. Parents owe it to the kids to give them the tools to compete, and those tools are often expensive. But they come before vacation,

the Harley, the leaf blower. If you don't want to sacrifice for your children, don't have them.

5. Parents should be available at all times for emergency talks. "All access," as the rock stars say. No excuses here. Ditch the meeting, get back from the mall, get off the phone. There is nothing more important than dealing with a child's crisis immediately, even if it seems trivial to the parent.

6. If a parent is looking out for the child, then that child's friends will be screened, the kid's whereabouts will be known at all times, and scholastic progress will be monitored daily. Homework will be looked at and questions about school will be asked. That's how trouble is spotted before it gets out of hand; that's how you bring out the best in your child. Children know you have a strong interest in their lives. They may bitch, but kids badly want that kind of attention. All the research shows that close parental monitoring is the leading factor in whether or not adolescents will engage in high-risk behavior.

7. Rules will be enforced but explained. Parents who truly look out for their kids understand that there are rules in society and that high standards of behavior are the key to a successful life. Rules are good. But rules must have a logical objective. "Because I say so" can

be effective when the kid gets stubborn, but before that conversation stopper is trotted out, try connecting some dots with your child. It doesn't always work, but the effort is worth it.

8. Parents will be honest at all times. Lead by example. No lying, no cheating, no nasty gossip, no cruelty, no manipulating, no jealousy toward your kids, no competing with them, no overindulging their various whims, and no overprotecting. Parents who are looking out for their children will prepare them for the rigors of this world. They will educate them **after** school, encourage generosity and spirituality, and generally do the right thing **all the time**. Or at least in front of them.

9. Parents will be respectful of **their** parents. Grandparent abuse or neglect is among the worst possible things a child can see. This is a very important commandment. You can't effectively look out for your kids if you don't look out for your folks. (Even if your folks don't deserve it.)

10. Finally, effective parents will remove the TVs and computers from their kids' rooms. All media absorption should be done in public space. This is a dangerous world, and the danger is now in the house. If a parent is really looking out for the kid, subversive material must be kept to an absolute minimum.

Corrupting influences on children are
everywhere, and parents must be full-time
firefighters. Life is tough and getting tougher.
The demons, the exploiters, want your kids.
You must look out for them. Fight hard.

Still true after all these years . . .
Agreed?

EIGHT

From SNL to The Daily Show, from Moveon.org to Occupy Wall Street . . .

It's All One Big Liberal Joke—and a Disturbing Pattern

In addition to the overwhelming liberal presence in print, TV comedians like David Letterman, Jon Stewart, and the cast of **Saturday Night Live** all lean to the left, as do their stables of gag writers. If you think such people are not important to the culture wars, you've been in a coma for the past ten years. Huge percentages of Americans, including many people in their twenties, report that they get much of their "news" from TV comedians. That might sound like a joke, but it's absolutely true.

It's also true that on any given night, TV political humor is spread all around the ideological spectrum. But do the body counts: It's the conservatives who are mocked the most. The cumulative effect of print and TV commentary that largely denigrates conservative thought and traditional values cannot be overestimated. It builds up in the minds of many Americans. It becomes huge.

Any questions?

But there's an antidote.

You guessed it: Fox News Channel, or FNC.

What I've written before is still true now. Some of the names below have changed—life moves on—but the theme is the same.

There is no question that FNC has a far more traditional feel than any other TV news network in America. Analysts like Sean Hannity, Brit Hume, and Charles Krauthammer generally approach issues from the conservative side, but there are also balancing voices on the left, like Alan Colmes, Geraldo Rivera, and Juan Williams.

And then there's me. While I am, perhaps, the strongest traditionalist voice on the FNC team, my perspective does not translate into conservative ideology. As anyone who watches **The Factor** knows, we scrutinize all the powerful all the time—no matter where their politics lie. . . . As everyone in the nation's capital knows, there is no political cheerleading on **The Factor** . . . period. We are watchdogs, not lapdogs.

———

Here's a simple account of my philosophy that I try to bring to TV every day. . . .

In the No Spin Zone we challenge people who don't directly answer the questions or purposely distort the facts. In order to impose the Zone rules, I have to interrupt when a guest begins to meander or, well, lie.

There are three reasons for this. First, I don't want to waste your time. Far too many TV interviewers allow their guests to blather on about nothing. Second, facts are facts—I have them in hand, and if the guest denies those facts, verbal confrontation immediately ensues. Finally, television is now run by computers. I have only so much time for each interview before the commercial break automatically appears on your screen. The machines have taken over.

I **have** to interrupt to stay on time.

It breaks my heart.

I'm spinning. It doesn't break my heart. I want people to GET TO THE POINT. I want them to be pithy. I want them to tell you the truth or what they think is the truth. I don't want bloviating, equivocating, or weaseling of any kind. Chatus interruptus is sometimes desperately needed on television.

Can I say "amen" to myself?

———

And look, if you're going to be in the spotlight every day, you're gonna hear your critics, but you don't always have to listen to them.

Your mother probably told you—mine told me— that you should never talk about religion or politics. And what am I doing every night? Making a career out of talking about religion and politics and everything else on the planet. For that, I take a massive amount of heat. . . . Fair enough. But like Harry Truman, I can stick it out in the kitchen.

Behind the refrigerator in that kitchen is often somebody like Barbara from Phoenix, who finds me personally offensive. "Mr. O'Reilly, you are rude, crude and unattractive. Nothing personal, just the facts as I see them."

Nooooo. Nothing **personal,** Barb. And if you think I'm unattractive on the tube, you should see me without makeup. Dogs howl. Bats fly in the daylight. Blowfish giggle.

———

You still believe nontraditionalists do not have an explicit agenda?

I guess you missed my exposure of the secular Ten Commandments about seven years ago. I'm not kidding. . . .

> ONE: Thou Shalt Not Make Any Judgment
> Regarding Most Private Personal Behavior.
> Man/Woman Is the Master/Mistress of
> the Universe and His/Her Gratification Is
> Paramount.
> TWO: Thou Shalt Not Worship or
> Acknowledge God in the Public Square, for
> Such an Exposition Could Be Offensive to
> Humankind.
> THREE: Thou Shalt Take from the Rich
> and Give to the Poor. No Private Property Is
> Sacrosanct.
> FOUR: Thou Shalt Circumvent Mother and
> Father in Personal Issues Such as Abortion and

Sex Education in Public Schools [see Chapter
Seven].
FIVE: Thou Shalt Kill If Necessary to
Promote Individual Rights in Cases of
Abortion and Euthanasia.
SIX: Thou Shalt Be Allowed to Bear False
Witness Against Thy Neighbor If That Person
Stands Against Secular Humanism.
SEVEN: Thou Shalt Not Wage Preemptive
War in Any Circumstance.
EIGHT: Thou Shalt Not Impede the Free
Movement of Any Human Being on Earth.
All Countries Should Be Welcoming Places
Without Borders.
NINE: Thou Shalt Not Prohibit Narcotics or
Impede Personal Gratification in This Area.
TEN: Thou Shalt Not Limit the Power of
Government in Order to Provide "Prosperity"
to All.

Yes. There **will** be a test.

————

But life is complicated. . . .

No one should long for "the good old days" of news
controlled by the powers of Washington, New York,
and Hollywood. Thanks to increased competition,

you are now much more likely to hear all sides of a story. Sometimes that's more information and more scandal than you might want to hear, but it's your right and your job as a citizen to face up to it. The news choices of today are an important change in your life. They help you decide what kind of country you want.

———

According to the polls, most Americans know the press is not looking out for them, since journalists are ranked near the bottom of all admired professions, right between lawyers and car salespeople. (By the way, nurses are ranked first.) The reason that we wretches are under so much suspicion is that we are perceived as being arrogant. That charge is tossed my way often. I'll let you make the call.

But there is no question that journalists, especially TV media people like me, are frowned upon by many Americans, and I understand. Despite my job, I am one of those Americans disgusted with a powerful press that refuses to report on the reality of everyday life in the USA. We have an obligation to demand accountability from big corporations that sell trash to kids. We have an obligation to report on school principals like the one in Plymouth County, Massachusetts, who refused to publicly discipline two students who engaged in oral sex on a school bus in full view of other young students. I mean, what kind of message does an educator send when he believes disgraceful public conduct is a private matter?

The fourteen-year-old girl and the sixteen-year-old boy who humiliated themselves and corrupted other children most likely got their oral sex education from the entertainment media (or President Clinton). We have an obligation to scrutinize show business and so-called "celebrities" who behave disgracefully. We have an obligation to hold the corrupters personally accountable.

But we are not doing it. And because of this cowardice and apathy, the forces of darkness are allowed to go to the bank unchallenged and, at times, even glorified. Worse still, when some of us in the press do object to the corporate assault on our culture, we come under attack ourselves because the elite media never, ever want to be shown up.

I'm not exaggerating; if you follow **The Factor,** you know that I am reviled in many media quarters and also in Hollywood. You will rarely see an article written about me that does not describe me as "contentious," "bombastic," "a blowhard," or "bullying." While that assessment may be accurate, couldn't they throw in an "incisive" or "courageous" or something like that once in a while?

Anyway, those adjectives are used only after the writer confers the label "conservative" on me. Why? Because in the world of the elite media, a conservative is someone who can be airily dismissed as a narrow-minded, predictable thinker. There are certain code words in the elite media's lexicon, and "conservative" leads the list.

———

Dealing with fear should be considered a traditional value, but few people actually do the work required.

I believe that overcoming fear is an essential key to living a useful and honorable life. Taming fear also trains a person to stand up to injustice. This is very important. When it is all over, when you are dead in the ground or in an urn, your legacy will be defined by two simple questions: How many wrongs did you right, and how many people did you help when they needed it?

That's it. Nothing more. No one will care how much money you made or what kind of car you drove. Those things don't inspire memorable eulogies.

So you can go ahead and hose people all day long, amassing great wealth and power, but what, exactly, does that mean? Nada, that's what. Note to the greed-heads and evildoers: You may be remembered for your misdeeds, but only as objects of ridicule or revulsion. On the other hand, the person who makes things better in this world will not be easily forgotten; his or her legacy will likely carry on. The good that you do in your life remains in the world.

But make no mistake: To attempt to right wrongs means conflict, and you will suffer. Most people are afraid of that suffering, so most people sit it out. My father was a role model in this regard, a good man afraid to stand up.

My core belief, as stated in my book **Culture Warrior,** is that life is a constant struggle between good and evil. That each person has free will and must choose a side. Refusing to choose puts one in the evil category by default, because bad things will then go unchallenged. The German people during the Nazi era demonstrated this better than anyone else. Most Germans were not Nazis, but most stood by and allowed incredible atrocities because they were either afraid or apathetic. Then they were forced to defend those atrocities by fighting World War II. Germany is still branded by that disgrace to this day.

But most evil is not as obvious as the work of Hitler and his pals, who flat out told the folks they were murderous racists. No, most bad people, out of cowardice or self-interest, attempt to disguise their evil. Some get justice, but some do not. For me, that's the most frustrating part of life: seeing evil individuals continue to harm people with impunity.

Keeping It Pithy

NINE

GETTING BACK TO TRADITIONAL VALUES

"The Code of the Traditional Warrior" and Other Top Hits

In my writings, TV talking points, and other bloviations over the years, I've often referred to traditional American values.

Just to be clear, I've broken my ideas on the subject down to ten **pithy** subjects. They define, I believe, a code for us to live by, if we choose.

1. Keep your promises.
2. Focus on other people, not yourself.
3. See the world the way it is, not the way you want it to be.
4. Understand and respect Judeo-Christian philosophy.
5. Respect the nobility of America.
6. Allow yourself to make fact-based judgments.
7. Respect and defend private property.
8. Develop mental toughness.
9. Defend the weak and vulnerable.

10. Engage the secular-progressive opposition in a straightforward and honest manner.

Almost 230 years ago the American Constitution enshrined these concepts—every one of them, if you look—in different words. (Thomas Jefferson might have had a paroxysm, a thing people used to do, over a term like "fact-based." But I think he'd get the point.)

I don't expect you to tape these ten subjects to your bathroom mirror.

But you could certainly do worse.

———

Speaking of traditional values . . .

Sex is supposed to be a private activity between consenting adults who are honest with each other, sharing pleasure and affection, and then shut up afterward.

Men, if a woman shares her body, take it as a gift of affection, not proof that you're stud of the month.

Ladies, if you said yes without being forced, then don't brag to your coworkers or your homegals.

———

By the way . . .

Researchers at Johns Hopkins have found that straining too heavily during sex can induce six to twelve hours of amnesia. This effect is called the Valsalva maneuver. So Clinton had a good medical excuse for his, uh, foggy grand jury testimony about his relations with Monica Lewinsky? And they weren't trivial, anyway. No. Under oath, there are **no** trivialities. By the way, what was the name of that maneuver again?

———

As you'll read in the last chapter, I've changed my mind about several different issues over the last few years.

One is gay marriage. I have not, as the president put it in his own case, "evolved." I've come to another conclusion, which you will soon read.

But I agree wholeheartedly with the following, written in 2000:

Dykes on Bikes? Take a hike! Can't you "express yourself" without throwing it in our faces?

When I'm walking down the street with a five-year-old, I don't want to have to try to explain why Jack is dressed up like Jill or Jill is wearing a buzz cut. The kid shouldn't have to be dealing with any sexual ideas at all, much less a couple of thousand folks marching around in drag or half-naked in order to "celebrate their sexuality." Give us all a break. Express your sexuality where the rest of us do, if we have any sense: at home, with the blinds drawn.

On the other hand, religious fanatics who demonize gays and other alternative groups aren't covering themselves with glory, either. Yes, I know about the references to homosexuality as "an abomination" in Leviticus, but I also know what the Old Testament says about slavery. As long as a sexual issue is not intruding on your freedom or endangering your kids, leave it to God to sort it out. The deity is a lot smarter than we are. That's also in the Bible.

Hold that thought. . . .

Tammy from Tennessee is fired up because I believe homosexuals should have equal protection under the law. "O'Reilly, why do you hate Christians? I believe the Bible is the word of God, and I take it literally. Homosexuality is an abomination to the Lord. Why are you so intolerant?"

Tammy, it is your right to believe in the Bible and live according to it. It is not your right to **impose** that belief on anyone else. I happen to believe that all Americans have a right to make a living and have a lifestyle free from religious judgment. As long as gays or any other group do not intrude on you, they should be left alone. Let God sort the private stuff out. He is smart enough to do it right.

Somewhat in this vein, a very interesting thing happened on **The Factor** with a story involving openly gay Ellen DeGeneres, J. C. Penney, and a conservative family organization known as One Million Moms. The background to the story is that the Moms demanded that the department store chain fire Ms. DeGeneres as a spokesperson because of her sexual orientation.

Here's a portion of my discussion of the topic on my program January 28, 2013, with Fox News contributor Sandy Rios. . . .

O'REILLY: This is a business deal. Ms. DeGeneres is hired as a spokesperson by J. C. Penney. J. C. Penney has an absolutely perfect right to do that. . . . So there she is, earning a salary to represent the department store chain. And then the Million Moms say, "Hey, because we feel a certain way about Ms. DeGeneres's lifestyle, you need to fire her." I don't think that's the spirit of America, Sandy, I've got to tell you.

RIOS: Bill, spokespeople stand for something. People are chosen because they stand for certain things. They represent companies. It matters very much what they stand for. From my perspective, it isn't about Ellen DeGeneres, but it's about mainstreaming something that is not acceptable to Christian and traditional family people all over the country.

O'REILLY: But they don't have to shop there. They don't have to shop there. . . . And this is where we run into a problem. Because if you remember with the McCarthy era, in the fifties, and they were hunting down communist sympathizers and not let them work . . . What is the difference between a McCarthy-era communist blacklist in the fifties and the Million Moms say[ing], "Hey, J. C. Penney and you other stores, don't you hire any gay people. Don't you dare"? What is the difference?

RIOS: The problem is that Ellen DeGeneres has chosen to act out her lesbian lifestyle, marry her partner. It is what that represents. And the fact that J. C. Penney is supposed to be middle America, the store where families shop . . .

O'REILLY: Don't shop there.

RIOS: It's disturbing to them.

O'REILLY: Don't shop there. . . . You're dodging the essential question. The essential question is that a group, a conservative group in this country, is asking a private company to fire an American citizen based upon her lifestyle. And I don't think that's correct. . . .

And so forth, round and round in the discussion, but I think you get my point.

———

Now, for something completely different—

Like Ann Landers, I've come up with a little manual for dealing with the opposite sex, but my point of view is not the same [as hers]. Bring on the cheek-to-cheek, the heavy petting, and the home runs, but not **ever** with any of the following prohibited, **ridiculous** lines:
He says,

"I've never met anyone like you." Please.

"You remind me of my mom." Run, lady.

"Sex isn't really that important." Run very fast.

"Look, I just want to talk to you. Nothing will happen if I come in." Lock the door.

"I haven't felt this way about a woman in years." If said on the first date, call the cops.

"Just one more drink won't hurt." Take his keys and drive home without him.

"Want to see my tattoo?" Begin coughing, and do not stop. Tell him you picked up something in the Amazon rain forest.

But it's not just the guys who come out with the ridiculous lines.

Your reporter has tirelessly collected a few gems from the other side:

She says,

"Let's be friends." Fine. Date her best friend.

"My sister's got two beautiful kids." Whatever you do, do not have sex with this woman.

"I'm not that kind of girl." Get the telephone number of her best friend right now.

"Where do you buy your clothes?" Get to a mirror fast.

"I'm **so** tired of the dating scene." Fella, she has **designs** on you.

"My ex-boyfriend . . ." She's still in love.

"When I graduated from Vassar . . ." Run.

"My mother says . . ." Run faster.

"Once I make up my mind about a guy . . ." Lock the door.

"I feel we have a soul connection." Dial 911.

"Christmas with my folks would be nice." That's it. Your dating days are done.

I see no reason to change any of the rules in my dating manual.
If you disagree, please let me know.

———

But, more seriously . . .
Many self-described traditionalists support the death penalty. We've all heard their arguments; they go back to the beginnings of the Republic.
This traditionalist disagrees.

I am against the death penalty because I feel it is too lenient a punishment. For example, Oklahoma City bomber Timothy McVeigh asked to be put to death and got his wish. McVeigh did not want to spend decades looking at the inside of stone walls and enjoyed going out as a martyr to his screwed-up confederates. According to some who corresponded with him, McVeigh almost relished the thought of the three different tubes of sedatives and poisons being dumped into his veins. And we accommodated him.

I've got a better idea. A punishment more appropriate—and much more terrifying—for McVeigh and others who commit crimes against humanity (this includes murder, rape, and large-quantity hard-drug dealing) would be to sentence them to life in prison in a federal penitentiary in Alaska. There they would be forced to endure hard labor, and if they refused to work, they would be quarantined in solitary confinement for twenty-three hours a day. This would effectively banish killers and rapists and condemn them to a life of harsh servitude. This is much more painful than death by injection or electricity.

There's another advantage, and we have to be honest about it. Mistakes can be made in criminal prosecutions for a variety of very human reasons. You've seen the reports about DNA or other evidence that has exonerated convicts, even some convicted of murder. It is going to happen because no system is perfect. By not executing prisoners a mistake like that can be rectified, as the convicts remain alive. (One interesting footnote: 53 percent of Americans in a national poll believe there should be an execution moratorium. That poll was taken in 2001 after some law students at Northwestern University produced evidence that some Illinois death row inmates had been improperly tried.)

But let's get back to you (and me).

A personal No Spin Zone will save you time, money, and frustration. It will allow you to make value judgments based upon hard facts and evidence. And—provided that you keep an open mind and examine all available credible data—you'll be comfortable with your conclusions on most matters.

Here's the key that unlocks the Zone: the ability to be rigorous with yourself in always challenging your initial thoughts and conclusions. The Zone is no place for zealots, lemmings, or weak-minded followers. It is a state of mind that demands the discipline of clear thinking and the flexibility to change that thinking should the evidence dictate. Summing up, the No Spin Zone is **not** an easy place to be.

Why? Because it's far easier to let others form your opinions. You then don't have to exercise your brain cells and the crowd will readily accept you. Politicians, commentators, and others vying to fill your head space are eager to supply you with particular points of view. And increasingly, many Americans are buying into viewpoints that crush independent thinking. Why think when media talking heads and newspaper columnists will do that for you? After all, aren't these people "experts"?

Well, no, they are not. At least most of them aren't. There are no experts when it comes to making personal decisions. That's your own private domain. Sure, nobody is right all the time and you won't be either. We are all occasionally defeated on the field of logic. But take your shot at forming your own personal philosophy. It's actually fun and satisfying to develop a code of behavior and a clear thinking pattern. Don't let pinheads, even smart pinheads, do your thinking for you.

———

Here are the outlines of my own personal No Spin Zone.

Yours will be, and of course should be, different. Last I heard, no two people are exactly alike.

I believe that the federal government wastes a huge amount of the people's money and that most politicians buy votes with entitlement promises.

I believe that global warming is real.

I believe that the green movement has hurt America because it has shut down responsible energy exploration.

I don't believe in the death penalty [see page 105].

I would not outlaw abortion, but I would restrict it and encourage Americans to see this ghastly procedure as a human rights issue.

I believe in stringent control of hard drugs, but I would decriminalize marijuana use.

I would "suggest" that the automakers develop cars and trucks that would be far more fuel-efficient than they are today. (If they don't, the government ought to slap a huge tax on them.)

I would order the Department of Energy to strictly monitor any kind of energy price collusion or gouging—and impose massive fines on any company found guilty of these crimes.

I would have the federal government negotiate discounted drug prices with pharmaceutical companies so that there could be an affordable Medicare drug benefit. These manufacturers should be pressured to be "generous" in their pricing and rewarded with tax incentives for complying.

I believe America should maintain the most powerful armed forces in the world and develop a missile shield if the technology is feasible.

I would eliminate the payroll tax and institute a national sales tax to cover Social Security and Medicare. The sales tax would slide depending on need. Those Americans who saved would be rewarded. The poorest would have more cash in their pockets.

I support setting up federal prison work camps on federal land in Alaska for violent offenders. Murder, rape, hard-drug dealing, and gun crimes would be punished at the federal level—taking the massive expense and chaos away from the states. These federal prisons would be run military-style, and the violent convicts would in effect be banished from society.

I believe our government should place the U.S. military on the border with Mexico to stabilize the illegal immigrant and drug smuggling problems. The military would back up the Border Patrol but would have arrest powers, requiring that the posse comitatus law be changed.

In conjunction with strict border enforcement, the USA should set up a "guest worker" program if the Mexican government would cooperate. U.S. companies and individuals that need labor would be able to participate in the program. But it would be administered in an orderly manner and taxes would be paid.

Your turn now.
Get cracking.

————

Rules for dealing with me.

I don't tolerate victimizers or charlatans or liars or manipulators.

If solicitors call my home, for example, I tell them within ten seconds that I do not do business on the phone—they can send me something if they like. Then I hang up. Rude? No. The **call** is intrusive and rude.

Another example is that I have instituted the two-call rule in my personal Zone. If I call a person twice and don't receive a call back, that relationship is over. I leave a short message saying that I will not be calling again. If it's a business matter, I turn the thing over to my attorney (an old friend I trust). If I absolutely have to reach someone for business, I call his or her secretary and set up a phone appointment. I ask for an exact time when I can talk to the person. If the secretary is unwilling to do that, I know that the business arrangement, whatever it is, will not work.

Other Zone Commandments.

If I've made a restaurant reservation, I expect it to be honored within fifteen minutes. Same with a doctor's appointment. The physician's time is valuable, but so is mine and so is yours. Being on time and honoring your word are signs of respect. I want to deal only with people who are respectful of others, even in a casual setting such as a restaurant. Be aware of how others are treating you and question that treatment if you feel it isn't square. That's all part of a no spin life.

———

What I've learned over the years is that friendship is a two-way deal, and it's not easy. People get married, have kids, get sick, lose jobs, live life. And to keep a friend through all that, you have to be accessible. Some of my friends check in regularly, some just once in a while. But I have to know that they are there if I need them. Because they know the converse is true.

Like everyone else, I've lost friends along the way. That is inevitable, and I don't dwell on it. If somebody vanishes, I'll try to find out why. But I won't try too hard.

That's because true friendship is a choice you make. Both parties have to buy in on an equal basis. If you have to convince someone to be your friend, the concept of friendship falls apart. Like love, you can't force it.

That's why my father said you're lucky to have five friends in your entire life. He had a few friends, but not many. My mother had far more, because she was outgoing and accessible, while my father was intense and often exhausted.

Sadly, I see the concept of friendship, as I have outlined it, declining in America. With people moving around so much, the small-town neighborhood culture we once had in this country is being replaced by high-tech anonymous "friendship" that's offered on the Internet. This trend will likely weaken the social fabric of the United States, as long-term friendships, like long-term marriages, are a societal stabilizer.

For me, old friends have made me stronger and happier. In my early years, I had no idea that I would rise so high in my career; nor did my friends. They were betting on the penitentiary. But we didn't base our friendships on the expectation of material success. Some of these guys have been with me in Levittown, at St. Brigid's, through high school and college, at my first journalism job in Scranton, Pennsylvania, and onward through the decades. Never did it matter what my job was or where I lived or how much money I made. It's always been, and still is, about shared experiences and loyalty. . . .

Summing up, friends don't let friends forget where they came from. Should be a commercial.

TEN

A DECADE'S WORTH OF HEAD SHOTS TO THE RICH AND POWERFUL

The Good, the Bad, the Ugly

Quite a few of you had never heard of **GEORGE SOROS** when I wrote about him in **Culture Warrior**. (So you told me.) But if you were awake during the 2012 election, you must have read or seen reportage about his huge financial support for his favorite left-wing causes.

Soros is El Jefe of the S-P forces, a man whose vast fortune is directed toward undermining traditional America and replacing it with a so-called Open Society. George Soros is the puppet master, the man with the plan, a ferociously far-left force about whom most Americans know little or nothing. . . . What kind of

man is Soros? Well, he does not believe in God, his social philosophy is libertarian, and his political outlook is far, far left. . . . At this point, he is the prime financier of a number of operations that consistently smear conservative and traditional Americans. . . . To sum up, Soros is a smart, ruthless ideologue who will stop at nothing to advance the secular-progressive offensive. He has no scruples, ethics, or sense of fair play.

———

On a lighter note, as they say, here's what I wrote once about S-P-leaning actor **ALEC BALDWIN**.

Alec Baldwin is a first-rate actor who can convincingly bring to life a variety of characters. Check out his performance in **Glengarry Glen Ross**. It's brilliant. Yet Baldwin has not achieved the leading-man fame that was once predicted for him, and some believe his strident politics (calling Dick Cheney a madman, generally overreacting to conservative thought) have damaged him in the marketplace because some

right-leaning Americans abhor his politics. And it might be true. . . .

Okay, okay.

You can stop laughing now. He's everywhere in the entertainment marketplace.

Stop it!

———

I'm the perceptive one, all right. Check this out.

CHARLES RANGEL. The congressman from Harlem may be to the left of Karl Marx, but he will show up anywhere  to defend his positions, and he does so with good humor. I always enjoy sparring with him, and I find that he is always worth listening to. Why? Because he is a hardscrabble guy who actually cares about his constituents. If we had more elected officials like him, from left to center to right of the political spectrum, this would be more like the country designed by our Founding Fathers. There's nothing wrong with having opposite points of view. What's wrong is corruption or incompetence.

Charlie, I guess we hardly knew ye.

We're all flawed. I say that a lot, always including myself.

But Rangel's apparent ethical "malfunctions" now being investigated are so petty, so stupid, so hurtful to his legacy that I'm flummoxed.

It takes a lot to flummox me. I still believe most of what I wrote above, but how can both Rangels exist in the same man?

If you figure it out, write me.

———

Somehow, when I talk about others, I often talk about myself as well.

Something wrong with that?

I am a journalist who insists on honest government; I'm an absolutist (some say fanatic) in that way. Lie, cheat, steal in the public arena—I'm gonna let you have it and I don't care who you are.

DAN RATHER is more of a pragmatist. He indeed has seen it all and is willing to tolerate far more shenanigans than I am. He understands that a certain amount of corruption is built into the system and is willing to play by those rules. I am not.

———

FOX NEWS EXCLUSIVE

Three times I have interviewed **GEORGE W. BUSH**, and here is my assessment: I believe he is an honest man. I believe his presidency was challenged by extraordinarily difficult circumstances that only a few other chief executives have ever faced. The terror attack on September 11 instantly changed the world, introducing a complex set of unique circumstances to Americans. Understanding that, I do cut President Bush some slack, unlike many in the media.

That being said, President Bush has made some major mistakes, most of which were exacerbated by what I call "the rich-guy syndrome." Let me explain. For people like me, raised in working-class homes, disaster is always in play, constantly present on the horizon. As I mentioned, both my mother and father were possessed by a nagging fear that stuff would inevitably go wrong. This is common among everyday folks who have to work hard to get by.

But Americans born into wealth and power usually do not have that fear. That's because things always seem to work out for them. Money buys security from harm and often can mitigate difficult situations. Power, as we've discussed, leads to opportunities. You must accept that truism in order to understand President Bush and his approach to vexing problems.

The crowning achievement of the Bush administration, usually ignored by the bitter left-wing media, is the hurt it put on al Qaeda. Within a year after 9/11, President Bush and his allies had delivered a series of devastating blows to the Islamic extremist community. The Taliban were routed in Afghanistan, dozens of al Qaeda leaders and operatives around the world were captured or killed, and scores of countries cooperated with America in freezing suspected terrorist bank accounts.

President Bush was flush with success. In most polls, his approval ratings were above 80 percent.

Then came the invasion of Iraq and the unraveling of the president's initial terror war success. As you know, the "Bush lied" crowd cannot stop screaming that the president fabricated the reasons for removing the tyrant Saddam Hussein. The prevailing wisdom on the far left is that Bush is a savage warmonger intent, for venal reasons, on imposing American dominance on the world. The anti-Bush partisans paint a harsh picture, and unfortunately, many people believe it. But that analysis is largely bull. . . .

Nonetheless, I have to agree with critics that the post-Saddam planning by the Bush administration was abysmal. Soon after Saddam was pushed from power, I told my audience that American forces were not nearly aggressive enough in controlling the looting that was taking place in Iraq. I was amazed and depressed by the chaos. Why wasn't this kind of lawlessness anticipated?

But, apparently, President Bush was not equally appalled. Furthermore, as subsequent events spiraled downward in Iraq, the president was very slow to react. Why? Well, my view is that he believed it would all **work out**. Again, that's the mind-set of rich guys. Everything will turn out okay because it has **always** turned out okay.

———

ROSIE O'DONNELL. Ms. O'Donnell has talent, she works hard, she's gathered a lot of loyal fans. But what's going on with the political stuff? Nobody should begrudge any American the right to an opinion, but, hey, Rosie, come on, let's think out your flaky liberal agenda a little. Are you making sense, or

are you spouting propaganda? I mean, a guy named Joseph Goebbels did the same thing on the very far right during World War II. Ms. O'Donnell demonizes anyone she disagrees with, and her musings are not to be questioned. But if you're gonna use your daytime soapbox to advance ideologies, Rosie, can't you at least allow someone with some knowledge to **question** you about it? (And I don't mean Tom Selleck.) I respect anyone with a well-thought-out opinion, but pure propaganda on national TV needs to be labeled for what it is. There are usually two sides to every issue. It is ridiculous to present only **your** side.

Back to the present: Her most recent TV outing did not work out, and she doesn't have Bush in the White House to kick around anymore, but I bet we haven't heard the last of her. There'll be another incarnation down the pike.

It is safe to say that JIMMY CARTER has used some of his power to avoid talking to me. About anything. He'll talk with Hamas killers, thereby legitimizing them in the eyes of some folks, but forget about conversing with the bold, fresh guy. I do take this personally.

Over the years, we've invited Mr. Carter on **The Factor** dozens of times, but his "people" barely returned our calls. When they did deign to, I believe there was some sneering going on. This despite the fact that President Carter seems to write a book every three weeks and will appear on cooking shows to promote his work. So there is no question in my mind that Carter does not "get" the bold, fresh guy (whose program sells tons of books for smart authors). Or maybe he does understand and simply despises me. That has been known to happen.

To be fair, President Carter is smart to avoid me, because I think he was a disaster as president. I think he's an okay guy, building those houses for Habitat for Humanity and such, but as the leader of America, the guy was scary. . . .

There is little more for me to say about Carter. During the hostage crisis, Iran made him look like Little Bo Peep, and on his watch, Americans had to line up for hours to get gas for their cars. Richard Nixon might have been a liar and a crook, but at least he had a clue about the real world and how it works. Carter was given power by the American people and rewarded their judgment by finishing his term looking like Swee'Pea from the Popeye comics. Some guys just can't handle life in the power lane. That was Carter.

—————

On the music front, **MADONNA** bugs me. Her early songs are catchy, and I like the fact that she came from humble Michigan roots before rising to the top of the charts. According to **Forbes** magazine, she's now worth about $350 million; quite an achievement for a working-class girl. But, somehow along the way, Madonna has succumbed to the awful disease of pretension. The latest symptom is her phony English accent. What is that all about? Is there no one alive who can tell Madonna that, when she talks these days, she sounds like a transsexual version of Peter Sellers? Annoying? Off the chart.

But did anyone care what I thought?
  Guess not.

Madonna's concert act in 2012 was number one in attendance in the world.

The weasels were waiting for BURT REYNOLDS, whom I covered during my Dallas [TV-reporting job] in 1977. He was shooting **Semi-Tough**. This was just after his famous seminude pictorial in **Cosmopolitan** magazine, when he was a regular on Johnny Carson's **Tonight Show** and was earning over $1 mil-  lion a year—an incredible sum at the time. Burt took full advantage of Dallas with hot and cold running babes in his hotel suite and fleets of limos. Crowds of fans appeared wherever he went. With that kind of treatment he could have been obnoxious to this young reporter dogging his heels, but he was actually very gracious and I kind of liked him. Once, he took the time to compliment me on a story I'd done about his costar, Robert Preston. But even I had enough smarts to see that he was headed for a fall. He was too cocky to the wrong people and had too many guys named Vinnie and Marty whispering in his ear. Six years later his career blew up after a series of unbelievably foolish racing car movies. Then he lost a dramatic amount of weight, which sparked wildfire rumors in Hollywood that he had AIDS. Actually the problem was linked to a jaw disorder, but the rumors crushed his leading-man status. He's never fully recovered. Quite simply, the press built him up, and the press tore him down.

I never enjoy telling stories like this one.

But they have to be told. Young people who overnight attain great public acclaim are even more vulnerable now than ever before, thanks to social media and vicious bloggers and ambitious hangers-on.

The weasels won't even leave the likely future queen of England alone when she's on a private holiday.

———

Take ELTON JOHN. He had to sell off the rights to most of his music when he got into debt up to his toupee. At the point where he had made more than $100 million, he was spending $400,000 a week, according to his accountant. Think of how many candles in the wind that would buy. We once shared a car in L.A. He was doing a private concert for King World, the company that owns **Inside Edition, Wheel of Fortune,** and **Jeopardy!** I was invited to the event because of my **Inside Edition** job. The car ride was truly bizarre. Trying to make conversation

with John was like trying to teach calculus to a gold-fish. Not going to happen. "Where are you living now?" I tried. My traveling companion ruminated for a few moments and finally decided he knew the answer: "Atlanta." This was news. "When did you move from England?" He became confused and said nothing. My final attempt was no more successful: "Which songs mean the most to you after all these years?" He looked as if he would throw up on my shoes. Out came very strange sounds, like the chorus to "Crocodile Rock." He buried his head in his hands. I spent the rest of the ride trying not to disturb an obviously distraught Elton. I learned one thing: Money can't buy good conversation.

Again and again, the celebrity is unreasonably treated like an expert on everything, but sometimes the shoe might fit, although in strange ways. A reporter for the **Weekly Standard** asked the very famous O. J. SIMPSON for his considered

opinion on President Clinton's problems with Paula Jones. His reply revealed the wisdom of a man with experience, I guess: "If it's true what happened to Paula Jones in that room with Clinton, then simply for hitting on a dog like her he should do thirty days. Other than that, I don't think it's anyone's business." Why didn't the White House put Mr. Simpson on the witness list for the Senate trial?

Let's move on. . . .

———

Okay, it's not even close: **OPRAH WINFREY** is the most powerful woman in the world. Sorry, Hillary. Born into deep poverty in 1954, this woman makes Bill Clinton look like Prince Charles in the humble-beginnings department. Compared to her upbringing in Mississippi, I was raised in the Taj Mahal. And even worse, Ms. Winfrey recalls being molested as a child by several male relatives and friends of her family.

Add it all up and Oprah's climb to the top of the power mountain is simply stunning. No other word for it. So what does this say about America, Michael Moore?

What kind of power does Oprah wield? Well, **Parade** magazine reports that she makes $260 million a year. That's about one million bucks for every day she actually works. Wow.

Basically, earning that kind of money means that Oprah Winfrey can do or buy anything she wants on this earth as long as it's legal and for sale. Like Lola in **Damn Yankees!,** whatever Oprah wants, Oprah gets. Think about that. There are no material limits for Oprah, nothing she cannot afford. Are you still thinking? Does Oprah's situation sound good? Okay, here's the downside: Having that kind of money can literally drive a person crazy.

Here's why. . . . Remember those glittering Christmas mornings when you were a kid? Mine were thrilling, the highlights of my childhood. The anticipation of getting fun stuff makes most kids happy for weeks. That's why Christmas is magic. Most children experience true joy during that season.

But it was the anticipation, the rarity of the experience that conjured up the magic. If, like Oprah, you can have Christmas every day of the year, there isn't much anticipation, is there? I mean, the thrill of obtaining something exceptional, or unexpected, or long awaited, just doesn't exist. With everything almost instantly available, everything becomes rather ordinary. For that reason, the ultrawealthy, if they are not ultracareful, can become bored, jaded, or, even worse, sadistic or self-destructive. The awful behavior of some celebrities and power brokers illustrates that point beyond a reasonable doubt. Just ask Caligula.

Meanwhile, Oprah has probably made a major career mistake by leaving broadcast TV and going to cable. She's not doing all that well, even after the blanket of publicity surrounding the Lance Armstrong interview.

Time will tell.

———

The beat goes on.

After the tragic school massacre in Sandy Hook, Connecticut, the gun control controversy seized the attention of the nation. Some people on both sides kept their cool, listened to each other, and tried to come up with rational answers.

One astonishing exception was the rash action taken by the **Journal News,** a paper in White Plains, New York. Using the Freedom of Information Act, reporters were able to collect tens of thousands of names of gun owners in three local counties—Westchester, Rockland, and Putnam—and publish them as a gun-owner database in map form online in December.

For about a month, newspaper executives explained that they felt they were doing the public a service. How's that again? Invasion of privacy? Giving potential gun thieves information they can use?

As one of the hundreds of people who called the newspaper to complain put it, "The implications are mind-boggling. It's as if gun owners are sex offenders [and] to own a handgun risks exposure as if one is a sex offender. It's crazy."

It was.

By mid-January someone came to his or her senses, and the map was deleted from the paper's website.

———

A lighter note on the continuing gun debate occurred on December 5, 2012, when a celebrity guest found himself caught in a controversy of his own making and came on my program to explain himself. As you'll see, I was glad to help him out. I think you'll be amused.

During a Sunday night football game, NBC's **BOB COSTAS** condemned what he called the gun culture in America. Some folks got angry because they felt the sportscaster was attacking the Second Amendment. He came to visit. . . .

O'REILLY: So first up, how do you feel about the right to bear arms?

COSTAS: Obviously, Americans have a right to bear arms. I'm not looking to repeal the Second Amendment. I haven't immersed myself in the issue throughout my life. I'm aware of it, as many Americans are. I didn't call for any specific prohibition on guns. I never used the words "gun control." I quoted from a column by Jason Whitlock, who was in Kansas City for a long time, now is on the Fox Sports website, in which he mentioned, I think credibly, a gun culture in this country. Now, it plays itself out in many ways, but it's a mentality about and toward guns that almost always leads to tragedy rather than safety.

O'REILLY: All right. And we'll get to that in a moment. But I think I want to clear this gun control thing up, because that's . . . that's why you got in trouble, because some people felt—

COSTAS: Yes.

O'REILLY: And this is a very emotional issue—

COSTAS: Of course it is.

O'REILLY: And the second thing, Mr. Whitlock is really, really far out there.

COSTAS: Well, I—I am not agreeing with—

[After some cross talk, we got back on track.]

COSTAS: In any case, I was unaware of [Whitlock's remarks comparing the NRA and the Ku Klux Klan]. And obviously, I would disagree with that 100 percent.

O'REILLY: Not scolding you, just—

COSTAS: I get it.

O'REILLY: I'm not scolding, I was trying to—

COSTAS: That's a mild scolding compared to what I've—

O'REILLY: Yes, I mean—okay.

COSTAS: —received over the last seventy-two hours.

O'REILLY: As long as you call a Christmas tree a Christmas tree, you're okay here.

COSTAS: Yes. Merry Christmas to you, too, Bill.

O'REILLY: All right. There you go. So let's advance the story a little bit. Gun control in America is an emotional issue because it is clear that the Founding Fathers gave the right to bear arms for two reasons. . . . Number one, because they felt that the government might devolve into tyranny, and the second thing was they knew that they had to settle this giant country and there weren't going to be laws out in the West and people had to have guns to protect themselves from bears and—Native Americans that didn't like them—

COSTAS: Yes. Yes.

O'REILLY: —coming on their property. So there's a history here, all right? And most people don't even understand that history. So Americans grow up with the right to protect themselves—against the government and against bad people. Then you enter into the modern age, where you have a debate about, well, what's the government's responsibility here, because these are lethal weapons? And that's where you come in, right? So you're saying that you want a more stringent program by the authorities to make it harder to get guns—

COSTAS: It sounds like you're saying I'm saying that.

O'REILLY: You're not saying that?

COSTAS: If you were to ask me, I believe that there should be more comprehensive and effective controls on the sale of guns.

O'REILLY: But what does that mean?

COSTAS: Roughly 40 percent of the guns purchased in this country do not require a background check for purchase.

O'REILLY: Okay. You want a background check, right?

COSTAS: You have that. You've talked about stricter penalties, harsher penalties for criminals. There is that. There ought to be training programs for those who purchase guns. I don't see any reason why someone should be able to purchase military-style artillery and body armor and automatic weapons. Only the police or the military should have that—

O'REILLY: All right, all of those are reasonable positions.

COSTAS: And none of that impinges on someone's Second Amendment rights or the right to protect their home and their family.

O'REILLY: You know what? I agree with most of that—but here is where you made your mistake. Are you ready for your mistake, Costas?

COSTAS: Yes, I'd like to hear it.

O'REILLY: All right, you're going to. Roll the tape.

[VIDEO CLIP]
COSTAS: It demonstrates itself in the Wild West/Dirty Harry mentality of people who actually believe that if a number of people were armed in the theater in Aurora, they would have been able to take down this nut job in body armor and military-style artillery, when, in fact, almost every policeman in the country would tell you that that would have only increased the tragedy and added to the carnage.
[END VIDEO CLIP]

O'REILLY: No, here's the deal. You and I are in a theater.

COSTAS: Yes.

O'REILLY: Okay, in Colorado.

COSTAS: Yes.

O'REILLY: We're watching the Batman movie.

COSTAS: Yes.

O'REILLY: The nut comes in through the back door—

COSTAS: Yes.

O'REILLY: —with his guns and he opens fire.

COSTAS: And his body armor.

O'REILLY: His body armor, whatever else he had, and he opens fire—

COSTAS: And this gun that can fire off hundreds of rounds—

O'REILLY: Right. And we're saying to ourselves, gee, I really don't want to get killed here. And you're seeing other people go down. Answer my question now. It's very simple—as you know,

I'm a simple man. Would you rather have the choice of ducking down on the floor or having a handgun on you to pull out and defend yourself against the man?

[The discussion goes back and forth for some time, with Costas evading my question. I try again.]

O'REILLY: You're evading my question. Bob Costas and Bill O'Reilly are in the theater. . . . Do you want to hit the floor and hope you don't get shot or do you want to have a gun on that you could protect yourself with?

COSTAS: I don't want—I don't want to have a gun on me—

O'REILLY: Okay. I respect that. You don't want a gun. I want one.

[We go around and around on the issue. Neither of us convinces the other. We part with respect.]

O'REILLY: Thanks for coming in here, Costas. It's good to see you, man.

COSTAS: Merry Christmas.

O'REILLY: Anytime you get in trouble, you come right here. We'll get you out of it.

COSTAS: Yes, I know you have security here.

O'REILLY: Lots of it.

COSTAS: Yes . . . They're armed, I assume.

That was a lot of fun for me, and I hope for Costas, too. We talked about one of the most important and divisive subjects of our time, but with mutual respect. That's the way it ought to be.

———

I've been doing **The Factor** now for more than seventeen years.

Can you believe it?

In that time I've changed a lot. I still get upset when people like Barney Frank lie to me on camera, but I'm more tolerant of harmless, dopey people and now pretty much just give you a wink.

You know what I'm thinking, so I don't have to say it.

And one more thing: I've changed my opinion in some matters.

And that leads us to the finale. . . .

ELEVEN

THE LAST WORD

(As Usual, I'm Taking It)

On February 7, 2013, I debated my pal Bob Beckel on the subject of President Obama's drone program that targets terrorists, killing them from the sky on presidential order. At issue was how the liberal media responded to the president's use of lethal force against suspected terrorists, as opposed to the way the left-leaning press discussed how President Bush allowed waterboarding.

The point is clear: The liberal media, including many at NBC News, were hysterical over waterboarding but rather muted when it came to **criticizing** the drone strikes. The reason is clear: The national media love President Obama and loathed President Bush.

In the body of the debate, I remarked that NBC News had said little or nothing about drones up until the congressional hearings that featured national security guy John Brennan. Beckel did not dispute that. We both understood that we were talking about the waterboarding-drone comparison.

After the segment aired, the left-wing media went wild. A variety of loons pointed out that I had not mentioned that NBC News had broken the "drone memo" story, which reported that President Obama's legal counsel had justified the policy. That was true: NBC was given the memo and aired it. It was also true that I did not mention that fact.

The left-wing media howled that I should apologize. I refused.

The reason is simple: We were not talking about reporting the drone situation. Beckel and I were talking exclusively about the analysis of waterboarding versus drones. On February 7, I pointed that out on **The Factor,** told the left-wing media to stuff it, and went my merry way.

Now, some might say that this is an example of O'Reilly never admitting to making a mistake. And they have a perfect right to see it that way. But I presented my case coherently and have the videotape to back it up. No apology or retraction was necessary.

The truth that every fair-minded person should understand is that NBC News and other left-leaning media operations have been extremely hypercritical in their analysis of American antiterror activities in general. That is a fact.

Despite a fair amount of bluster on my part, the truth is also that I do change my opinions from time to time. I must point out, however, that before I bloviate on TV about an issue, my staff does heavy research on it. I always want to be armed with the facts because

I well know that everything I say is fodder for my enemies. We must protect **The Factor**'s flanks with solid research, and we do.

It also takes facts to induce a change of mind on my part. And here are three examples of where that happened (there are many more).

The presidential election of 2012

- After the conventions, I was convinced that Mitt Romney would defeat Barack Obama. The governor was raising big money, the economy was weak, and the president looked to be exhausted by the stress of his situation.
- Up until eight days before the vote, I still believed Romney would carry the day.
- Then Hurricane Sandy blew Romney away.
- For five solid days, the governor disappeared from the national news cycle. But not President Obama. He was everywhere in the Northeast. Running around with New Jersey governor Chris Christie, showing empathy, promising help. Casual voters saw an engaged president.
- Nobody saw Romney.
- The Friday before Election Day, the polls were swinging the president's way. My producers were trying to convince both candidates to come on **The Factor** for extensive interviews. I actually talked with the head of the Obama campaign, David Axelrod, myself. He was honest: No way was the president going to interview with me be-

cause I would ask him about Libya. Also, Axelrod said, "we" were going to win. "We" didn't need to do a **Factor** interview.

- Axelrod knew what I knew: The internal polling showed a solid shift toward the president.

- The Romney people should have known that as well, but, apparently, they did not. I talked with a number of folks, including Ann Romney, and they gave me the runaround. They never said why the governor would not come on **The Factor**. He just never showed up, even though we would have given him a full thirty minutes the night before the election to make his case to the voters.

- Armed with that knowledge, I told **Factor** viewers that I could not call the election even though guys like Dick Morris and Karl Rove were saying Romney would win big. I wasn't sure Barack Obama would win, but I was certain it would be close. So I declined to make a call.

- In this case I changed my mind about the situation based upon facts. It was a smart and honest move.

The Iraq war

- At first I supported the action based upon Saddam Hussein's defiance of weapons inspections. I had little problem telling the folks that I thought the USA had to remove him because he was a loose cannon (pardon the pun) in the vast world of terrorism.

- But in hindsight, I had too much faith in the Bush administration's ability to think the Iraq campaign through. After the initial military victory by coalition forces, Iraq descended into mass chaos and the Bush people had no clue how to respond. When I traveled to Iraq in 2006, I saw that firsthand.

- The U.S. military, of course, snatched victory from the jaws of defeat, and for that I am extremely grateful—and you should be, too. The men and women who served in Iraq (and Afghanistan) are true patriots.

- But in hindsight, the campaign was not worth the blood and treasure. We could have removed Saddam another way. The carnage that took place in Iraq should have been avoided. I hope we have learned from that awful situation.

Gay marriage
- My basic belief is that the deity will sort out the personal stuff. If you are not hurting other people, you should be left alone to live your life. I don't care about the private lives of other individuals.

- However, I do believe that there are certain societal stabilizers and that the traditional family unit is one of them. Nature dictates that men and women procreate, and together they are mandated to raise children in a responsible way. That is the optimum in my opinion.

- Secular people see it differently. They believe that traditional marriage should be expanded to include gays, and if you don't do that, you are violating their rights. But marriage is not a "right." It is a sacrament in some religions and a category for the census.
- Thus I was never on board the gay marriage train.
- But after watching this never-ending debate, I have come to the conclusion that gay marriage should be left to the individual states to decide. There is no moral aspect to it that affects the country as a whole. Traditional marriage should remain the standard, but in our secular age, the legal system is not going to prevent gay marriage. Only a vote by the folks can do that, and even the will of the people will be subject to the Supreme Court.
- I support all popular votes. The folks should always decide what kind of environment they want as long as it does not harm other folks or violate the Constitution. I still do not see gay marriage as a "civil rights" issue. But I don't think it will harm America or the states that approve it.

———

Summing up, I am the exact opposite of Boy George's lyric "I'm a man without conviction. I'm a man who doesn't know." I do know. Not everything, but a lot. And my convictions have led to a satisfying career in journalism.

I hope reading this book has been entertaining and instructive for you. I know that sometimes I come off as "all about me." But I think you know that's not why I am in business. It's about you.

Thanks again for reading **Keep It Pithy**.

Photo Credits

Family Agency, Copyright © 1943 The Norman Rockwell Family Entities)

p. 39. **Nativity Scene** (Public Domain)

p. 43. **Thomas Jefferson,** Charles Wilson Peale (Public Domain)

p. 49. **Mass** (Public Domain)

p. 60. **Hillary Clinton** (Mark Wilson/Getty Images News/Getty Images)

p. 67. **"Captain" Lou Albano** (George Napolitano/ FilmMagic/Getty Images)

p. 69. **Steve Allen** (Steve Allen, June 1962/AP Photo)

p. 72. **SAW Poster** (Courtesy of Photofest Digital)

p. 74. **BLOW Poster** (Courtesy of Photofest Digital)

p. 79. **Bette Davis** (Public Domain)

p. 90. **Fox News Channel Logo**

p. 117. **St. Brigid's School** (Author's Collection)

p. 119. **George Soros** (Sean Gallup/Getty Images News/Getty Images)

p. 120. **Alec Baldwin** (Dario Cantatore/Invision/AP Photo)

p. 121. **Charles Rangel** (Susan Walsh/File/AP Photo)

p. 122. **Dan Rather** (Bebeto Matthews/AP Photo)

p. 123. **Fox News Exclusive**

p. 126. **Rosie O'Donnell** (Damian Dovarganes/File/ AP Photo)

p. 127. **President Jimmy Carter** (Charles Sykes/AP Photo)

p. 128. **Madonna** (Evan Agostini/AP Photo)

p. 129. **Burt Reynolds** (Scott Harrison/Archive Photos/Getty Images)

p. 131. **Elton John** (Joseph Okpako/WireImage/ Getty Images)

p. 132. **O. J. Simpson** (AFP/AFP Collection/Getty Images)

p. 133. **Oprah Winfrey** (Michael Tran/FilmMagic/ Getty Images)

p. 135. **Fox News**

ABOUT THE AUTHOR

BILL O'REILLY, a three-time Emmy Award winner for excellence in reporting, served as national correspondent for ABC News and as anchor of the nationally syndicated news magazine program Inside Edition before becoming executive producer and anchor of Fox News's breakout hit The O'Reilly Factor. He is the author of the mega-bestsellers **The O'Reilly Factor, The No Spin Zone, Who's Looking Out for You?,** and **Culture Warrior**, as well as **Kids Are Americans Too, The O'Reilly Factor for Kids**, and the novel **Those Who Trespass.** He holds master's degrees from Harvard's Kennedy School of Government and Boston University.

LIKE WHAT YOU'VE READ?

If you enjoyed this large print edition of
KEEP IT PITHY,
here is one of Bill O'Reilly's latest
bestsellers also available in large print.

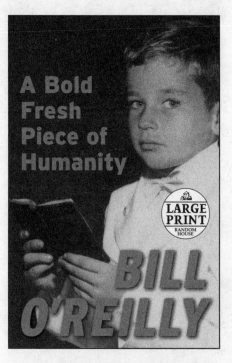

A Fresh Bold Piece of Humanity
(paperback)
978-0-7393-2800-2
($26.00/$30.00C)

Large print books are available wherever books
are sold and at many local libraries.

All prices are subject to change. Check with your
local retailer for current pricing and availability.
For more information on these and other large print titles,
visit www.randomhouse.com/largeprint.